GOD, SCIENCE AND THE BIBLE

GOD, SCIENCE AND THE BIBLE

*Genuine science confirms
the Bible's amazing message*

ARNOLD V PAGE

 Books for Life Today ™

© Arnold V Page 2020, 2023

2nd edition ISBN: 978-1-915283-04-7

COPYRIGHT NOTICES

The right of Arnold V Page to be identified as the author of this work has been asserted by him in accordance with The Copyright, Designs and Patents Act 1988.

Except as provided by The Copyright Act 1956, The Copyright, Designs and Patents Act 1988, and The Copyright and Related Rights Regulations 2003, no part of this publication may be reproduced, stored in a retrieval system, or transmitted in any form or by any means without the prior written permission of the copyright owner.

Revised Standard Version
Unless otherwise indicated, Bible verses are taken from the Revised Standard Version of the Bible, © 1946, 1952 and 1971, the Division of Christian Education of the National Council of the Churches of Christ in the United States of America. All rights reserved.

The Living Bible
Bible verses marked 'TLB' are taken from The Living Bible, copyright © 1971. Used by permission of Tyndale House Publishers Inc., Carol Stream, Illinois 60188. All rights reserved. The Living Bible, TLB and The Living Bible logo are registered trademarks of Tyndale House Publishers.

Figures 1 to 4: © Arnold V Page, 2020, 2023.

NOTE ABOUT SPELLING

British spelling (e.g. 'centre', 'defence', 'favourite', 'judgement', 'sceptical') has been used throughout.

God, Science and the Bible is an expanded edition of the first half of *Z: The Final Generation*, which was published in 2018 by the Westbow Press.

 Books for Life Today ™
86A Totteridge Lane, High Wycombe, HP13 7PN, England
Website: booksforlife.today
Email: sales@booksforlife.today

Preface

People used to say that you have only to look around you to know that God exists. They'd say that only someone far greater than us could have created everything, therefore there has to be a God. But then we were told that life as we know it evolved bit by bit from something far simpler without God's help, and that even the physical universe evolved from some inexplicable explosion of concentrated matter and energy without the help of any guiding hand. So now a quarter of the UK's population no longer believes in God's existence, and many more don't know what to believe.

Does it matter if people don't believe in God any more? Well, it might not matter to you if you have survived abortion, abandonment, bullying, abuse, theft, mugging, rape, marital infidelity, scams, slavery, terrorism, stabbing and murder by a population that no longer believes in the God of the Bible and therefore has no respect for his commandments. In fact not believing in God might not matter at all if there were nothing beyond this mortal life. Saint Paul wrote, *'If for this life only we have believed in Christ, we are of all men most to be pitied.'* (1 Corinthians 15.19)

But what if there *is* something more than life as we know it? What if this life is supposed to be only a preparation for proper life, a life that will surpass this life as your current mortal life surpasses the brief dark time you spent in your mother's womb? And what if this proper life to come is only for people who believe in God, or at least for people who would believe in him if they knew about him? In that case believing in God would be a matter of life or death.

As I write this preface, the EuroMillions lottery jackpot stands at £167 million or US$205 million. I've just bought a ticket for it. I've never bought one before and I'll probably never buy one again. But suppose it were a paper ticket and I threw it away, deciding it was probably worthless. If it had the winning numbers on it, that would probably be the worst mistake I ever made!

God has told us through his son Jesus Christ that something far better than the EuroMillions jackpot is on offer, and it's free of charge because Jesus paid for it with his life. *'For the wages of sin is death, but the free gift of God is eternal life in Christ Jesus our Lord.'* (Romans 6.23) God is offering us the prize of never-ending life in a recreated earth no longer spoilt by sin, decay and death. But Jesus said it is only for those who believe in God. *"He who hears my word and believes him who sent me, has eternal life; he does not come into judgment, but has passed from death to life."* (John 5.24)

Therefore if what the Bible says is true, believing in God and in what he says *does* matter. It matters more than anything you can possibly think of. So whatever you believe right now, come with me on a journey through the rest of this book. Let's find out together why genuine science—based on scientific laws and evidence rather than mere speculation—confirms God's existence and the truth of what the Bible tells us about him. Let's discover what the Bible really says about God's amazing purpose in creating us, and let's seize hold of it for ourselves.

Please don't end up gnashing your teeth when the results are announced on the day of judgement and you discover that you threw your ticket away too soon.

Arnold Page, High Wycombe, 2024

Dedication

I want to dedicate this book to Ann, my darling wife, who left this world soon after the first edition was finished. She had total faith that God wanted me to write it, and she willingly allowed me all the time I needed to do so. Her prayers and encouragement kept me going to the end. If you or anyone else puts their trust in God for everlasting life as a result of reading *God, Science and the Bible*, it will be due to Ann as much as to me.

God, Science and the Bible

Contents

Preface v
Introduction 1
1. Is there a God? 5
2. The Evidence of Design 11
3. The Evidence of the Resurrection 35
4. The Evidence of Experience 49
5. Six Thousand Years and Six Days 57
6. The Universal Flood 69
7. The Fossil Record 77
8. The Ages of Rocks and Trees 89
9. The Bible as the Word of God 99
Epilogue 113
Annex 1: Seven Days of Expanding Time 123
Annex 2: Fifty-day Bible-reading Plan 129
Other books by Arnold V Page 133

List of figures

Figure 1: The geological column, simplified 81
Figure 2: Growth ring chaining 96
Figure 3: Growth ring matching (1) 96
Figure 4: Growth ring matching (2) 97

List of tables

Table A.1: Comparison of calculated and accepted dates for the formation of the world   126

God, Science and the Bible

Introduction

What could it be?

"I AM GOING TO SPEAK TO YOU, but first I want you to pray that you'll understand what I say."

I was about to begin my morning Bible reading in the office I shared with José Pulgar, the Methodist Minister in Punta Arenas. Situated beside the Straits of Magellan, Punta Arenas is the most southerly city on the South American mainland. It was an important seaport before the Panama Canal was built. Nowadays, it's a major stop-off for cruise ships on one of the world's most scenic voyages. It is where I was living with my young family back in 1980.

All at once those words came into my head, as clearly as if I had heard them aloud. "I am going to speak to you..." Weird. Exciting. Awesome, even. *All right, I'd better do as I'm told.*

"Lord God, please help me to understand what you are going to say."

I waited. Nothing. The line had gone dead.

I decided to read the Bible passage set in the day's Bible-reading notes. It was a story Jesus told about a man who had no food in his house to offer to an unexpected guest.

Although it was late at night, the man cheekily knocked on his neighbour's door to ask him for some bread.

Knock. Knock.

"Who's there? What do you want?"

"It's me, Zak. Can you let me have a loaf of bread?"

"What? No, I can't. We're all in bed. Go away. Come back in the morning if you must."

"I can't. I've got a visitor and nothing to give him. I can't send him to bed hungry."

(Hospitality was a big thing in those days.)

"That's your fault. Go away, or you'll wake the kids up. I'm not getting out of bed for you, do you understand?"

KNOCK, KNOCK.

"Oh, for goodness' sake! All right, I'll give you what you're asking for."

I scratched my head. (Actually I didn't scratch my head, but you know what I mean.) Was God trying to say something to me through this? Was there something I had asked for without success, something he wanted me to ask for again? What could it be?

An amazing offer

Don Double, the founder of what was then called the Good News Crusade, had written to tell me that he and his fellow evangelist Mike Darwood were going to visit the Chilean capital, Santiago. He asked if I would like to meet them there. José suggested that I invite them both to come to Punta Arenas instead.

"Foreign missionaries never come down here," he said.

Don agreed, and I set to work recruiting the leaders of all the evangelical churches in the city to help prepare for a major four-day interdenominational event in which their members could participate. The church buildings all being on the small side, we sought other venues. We tried two sports halls, a small theatre off the main square, and even the main Municipal Theatre, but all were booked for other events. And now we had a problem: Don's and Mike's visit was only a fortnight away!

I thought again about the Bible reading. Of course! That must be what God meant. We were to ask again for one of the venues where we'd previously been turned down. All right, which was the best one? (The Lord must love it when we finally work out what he's getting at!) There was no question in my mind that the Municipal Theatre was the number one choice. It was large and central with car parking space, and it had comfortable seats.

I explained to José what I believed the Lord was telling me to do.

"We have to ask again if we can have the Municipal Theatre," I said. "We need it for four evenings, Thursday to Sunday."

"I think the Mayor might be the person to speak to," José told me.

"Will you speak to him? Your Spanish is better than mine."

Introduction

There was no way I was going to try persuading a Roman Catholic mayor, who probably wouldn't even approve of our evangelizing his citizens, to change his mind.

José returned from the telephone.

"I spoke to the Mayor," he said. "He asked me what we wanted it for, and he had a look in the diary. He said the theatre is booked for the Thursday and Friday evenings, but Saturday and Sunday are free, so we can have the theatre for those two days at least. What's more, he says we can have it free of charge as his contribution to the crusade!"

In the end we held the first two meetings in the Methodist Church, which was quite big enough, and the two main meetings in the theatre, which was nearly full. I'll tell you more about that later.

Ask again

Most of us at some point in our life ask some pretty important questions. Is there more to life than this? Does human life have any purpose other than its continuing existence? What is my own purpose in life? Is there a God, and if so can we know him... or her? Is the Bible true, or is the Qur'an true? Is there anything beyond death? Will Jesus really return as he promised? What about evolution and the Big Bang theory? What is the future of our planet?

We may not put such questions into spoken words, but I'm pretty sure that most of us ask them in our heads at least. We ask them and we either decide they're unanswerable or we accept whatever answers seem to be the most likely. We probably base such answers on what most people believe, or else on what seems most reasonable in the light of whatever we've read or been told. Fair enough.

But what if there *are* answers to all these questions, true answers that will revolutionize our lives when we discover them? Like Dr Ignaz Semmelweis's discovery that surgery should be carried out in antiseptic conditions? Or the discovery by Jesus's disciples on the first Easter Day that he was alive again and that they too could live forever if they would commit their lives to him?

I don't know how you have answered questions like those above. You may have decided that a belief in God is not essential.

Whether you regard yourself as a Christian or not, you may have adopted a number of beliefs that are contradicted by the Bible. You asked the questions once, and you answered them as best you could. But perhaps you are not entirely, totally, completely sure that you got the answers right. All I am asking you to do is what I did back in Punta Arenas: *ask again*. Try to put aside your current answers for the moment, and consider the possibility of some different ones.

According to Saint Mark, Jesus's opening words were, *"The time is fulfilled, and the kingdom of God is at hand; repent, and believe the good news."* (Mark 1.15) I believe that the kingdom of God is indeed at hand. I didn't always, but I do now. I changed my mind. That's what the Greek word translated 'repent' literally means: 'change your mind.' And it's what I'm asking you to do, if what you believe doesn't yet match what is in the Bible, because Jesus said that what is in the Bible is true. (John 17.17) If you really believe that what God says in the Bible is true, your whole life will change. You'll come into a personal relationship with God now and start to live the way you were always meant to; and eventually, when God recreates the earth in its original perfection and Jesus at last reigns as king, you'll live with him there forever. (John 8.36; 10.10; 14.19; Revelation 21.1-5)

It may be that God is saying to you what he once said to me: "I am going to speak to you, but first I want you to pray that you'll understand what I say." Will you do it?

1. Is there a God?

Does God exist?

> *The White Rabbit put on his spectacles. "Where shall I begin, please your Majesty?" he asked.*
> *"Begin at the beginning," the King said gravely, "and go on till you come to the end: then stop."*
> *Alice's Adventures in Wonderland*, Lewis Carroll

Let's begin by trying to answer the question, "Does God exist?" If your immediate answer to that question is "No", then I hope I can at least change it to "Don't know." If it is "Don't know", I'll try to move it in the direction of "Yes." And if it is already "Yes", then read on to learn how better to answer those who question *why* you believe in God. Wherever you stand on this question, I'm convinced you are about to read things you've never thought of before!

In this short chapter I want to tackle briefly what I think are two arguments that people use *against* any belief in God's existence, namely the evils of religion and the problem of pain. Other arguments about how a God of love could have destroyed the world in a flood, or command Joshua and his army to destroy the indigenous inhabitants of Canaan, or possibly threaten punishment in hell for those who reject him, are not arguments against the existence of God but against his perceived injustice. That is a different kind of question. I thought some of my schoolteachers were extremely unjust to me, but unfortunately that didn't stop them existing. Such arguments are not about God's existence but about his nature, so I won't address them here, but I will touch on them later.

Religion

Like other human inventions, religion can be a force for good or evil. People who believe it is mainly a force for evil tend to conclude that believing in God is evil and that therefore God does not exist. I'm not sure that this argument is logical., nevertheless the fact remains that some people find religion an obstacle to belief in God, so I need to address this matter in case you are one of them.

It has been said that more people have been killed in the name of God than for any other reason. Certainly religion has been responsible for some wars, but the number of deaths that have actually been caused primarily by religion is tiny compared with deaths from warfare in general. The *Encyclopedia of Wars* lists 1763 historical wars, of which only 123 or 7% have been identified as motivated primarily by religion.[1] Ancient wars, most mediaeval and Renaissance wars, the Napoleonic campaign, the American Revolution, the French Revolution, the American Civil War, World War I, the Russian Revolution, World War II, the conflicts in Korea and Vietnam, and most recently Russia's invasion of Ukraine—none of these was religious in nature or cause. And what about plagues, like the Black Death that killed a third of Europe's population in the fourteenth century; or hunger, which kills around 9 million people every year? The statement that more people have been killed in the name of God than for any other reason is totally untrue.

It is true that religions have been responsible for some hideously barbaric practices, such as the burning of children as sacrifices to the god Moloch by the local inhabitants during the period of the Hebrews' conquest of Canaan, gruesome tortures during the Spanish Inquisition, and in recent years the terrorist bombings and atrocities committed by ISIS in the name of Allah.[2] Such practices certainly bring some religions, or at least their devotees, into question, but not the existence of God, even if they claim to worship him.

If I were to start a religion based on worshipping King Charles III of Great Britain, and if I then taught my followers to kill everyone who wanted to abolish the British monarchy, that wouldn't mean that Charles suddenly ceased to exist.

---

[1] *Encyclopedia of Wars, Facts on File.* A.Axelrod & C.Phillips, Richard Deem, November 2004.

[2] http://www.mirror.co.uk/news/world-news/isis-release-chilling-video-english-7310064. Viewed June 2023.
While most Muslims would denounce the activities of ISIS as being nothing to do with true Islam, the ISIS leaders themselves believe that they are acting in the name and will of Allah.

In reality religion has been responsible for infinitely more good in the world than evil. In an extraordinary book entitled *An Atheist Defends Religion: Why Humanity Is Better Off with Religion Than Without It*, Bruce Sheiman produces countless arguments for the benefits of religious belief—whether or not God exists![3]

Sheiman's arguments apply particularly to the benefits that the Christian faith has brought into the world. Strictly speaking, Christianity is not a religion at all. Religions generally consist of rules and rituals invented by men to seek the favour of whatever notion of God their adherents may have. Basically Christianity is not about rules and rituals, neither is it of human invention. It's about a personal relationship with God, a God who initiated such a relationship by coming to the earth in the person of his Son Jesus, to meet us where we are. Unlike other religions, Christianity is not an attempt to win God's favour by fulfilling rules and rituals. It is a grateful response to his love for us, which we express by living as he intended us to live with the help of his Holy Spirit. And this Christianity and this faith began changing society for the better from its very beginning.

Paul's statement, *'There is neither Jew nor Greek, there is neither slave nor free, there is neither male nor female; for you are all one in Christ Jesus'* (Galatians 3.28), was a direct challenge to first century society. Jews and non-Jews hated each other; the Roman Empire's 60 million slaves were regarded as living tools to be thrown out once they were too sick or too old to be useful; women had no rights at all; and girl babies were often left in the street to die or to be picked up for later use in someone's brothel. A man could divorce his wife for adultery, drunkenness, or merely for making copies of the household keys.[4] A divorce could be formally granted on the request of one spouse even if the other was not informed.[5]

As the Christian faith took hold of people's minds and hearts, Jesus Christ's respect for non-Jews, slaves, women, children, the sick

---

[3] *An Atheist Defends Religion: Why Humanity Is Better Off With Religion Than Without It*. B.Sheiman, Alpha Books, 2009.

[4] *The long good-bye.* B.Holland & L.Yerkes, Smithsonian 28, no. 12: 86, March 1998.

[5] *Divorce Roman Style: How easy and how Frequent was it?* S.Treggiari in *Marriage, Divorce, and Children in Ancient Rome*, Ed. B.Rawson, Oxford University Press, 1991.

and infirm and for marriage revolutionized the ancient world. Christians founded hospitals, schools and universities for men and women. In Great Britain, many of the oldest and most famous hospitals, university colleges and schools are named after Christian saints because they were founded by Christians in the conscious service of Christ. The founding fathers of the USA were mainly practising Christians who wanted their national life to reflect Christian principles. If I understand correctly, their decision to separate religion and state was primarily to prevent the state interfering with religious faith rather than vice versa. In the eighteenth and nineteenth centuries, Christians in the British parliament led the fight against slavery, and even today Christian charities such as World Vision, Habitat for Humanity, Christian Aid and Caritas are among the world's leading aid and development agencies. I would argue that it is because British society and British values have been shaped by the Christian faith that even today Great Britain is the chosen destination of many refugees and economic migrants from North African and Arab countries.

Religions have occasionally been responsible for wars and other evils, and some still are today, but that is no reason at all not to believe in God!

The problem of pain

A second major reason that some people don't believe in the existence of God, or at least in the existence of a loving God, is what C.S.Lewis called 'the problem of pain'. (Lewis is most famous for his children's stories about Narnia.)

Human suffering is often terrible, but it is simplistic to blame it all on God. Natural disasters and diseases do cause suffering and death, and mental and physical handicaps can make life very difficult for the people concerned and their carers, but the vast majority of human suffering is caused by human beings. Warfare, violence, tyranny, corruption, terrorism, injustice, oppression, slavery, crime, starvation, homelessness, family breakdown, abuse of all kinds and many other evils are all caused by human beings. They are the result of man's selfishness, greed, laziness, dishonesty and cruelty, in other words what the Bible calls *sin*. Even the effects of natural disasters like earthquakes and floods would be greatly lessened if people made more of an effort to build safely and if wealthier countries helped poorer countries to do this. In January 2010 an earthquake in Haiti killed an estimated 230,000 people. Only two weeks later an earthquake *500 times more powerful* struck the coast of Chile affecting a similar number of people, yet the death toll amounted to only 525. Similarly, many diseases are caused by malnutrition, contaminated water, gluttony, alcohol consumption, lack of medication, and sexual promiscuity: all with causes and solutions that are in our own hands. We cannot demand to be independent of God, and then blame him for the consequences.

Secondly, if it is hard to believe in the existence of a good and loving God because there is so much suffering in the world, it should be equally hard to believe in the existence of an evil and hateful God when there is so much love, kindness, goodness and beauty in the world. Would an evil God create a mother who risks her life to save her child, or allow the founder of an international IT organization to donate billions of dollars to eradicate disease, or produce volunteer aid workers who daily risk their lives to take supplies into towns under enemy attack and to attend the victims of cluster bombs even as they are falling?

Sunshine and rain, earth and sky, trees and flowers, food and drink, above all our amazing minds and bodies—all these are blessings that God freely gives for our benefit or use every day. Put all these blessings and more into the scale pan of God's existence before you conclude that suffering tips the balance against belief in a good and loving creator.

Thirdly, our view of suffering is completely distorted so long as we think that human life is limited to 80 years or so in our current bodies. If a baby's life were limited to nine months of an uncomfortable existence in its mother's womb, it could rightly complain about the cruelty and meaninglessness of life. And if this present earthly life were not the essential preparation for an eternal life in a world that will be unbelievably better than anything we can imagine, then sickness, pain, mental and physical handicaps, and even death would indeed be hard to reconcile with the purposes of a loving creator. But if such sufferings are a necessary reality in a world that the Bible tells us has been damaged because of sin, and if nevertheless they are somehow intended to prepare us for something far better that is going to last forever, then any defiant outcry against the idea of a God of love shrivels into a snivelling whimper.

"Are we there yet?" is the universal cry of children who hate long, boring car journeys, but they know in their hearts that the journey will have been worthwhile when it ends at their holiday destination. Several of the New Testament writers urge us to adopt this same viewpoint when we suffer. Paul suffered far more than most of us will ever do, but he had no complaints. *'I consider that the sufferings of this present time are not worth comparing with the glory that is to be revealed to us,'* he wrote. (Romans 8.18)

Having tried as best I can to deal with two major obstacles *against* belief in God, it is time now to consider evidence *for* his existence.

2. The Evidence of Design

Three kinds of evidence

The classical case *for* God's existence falls into three parts:[6]

- the evidence of design
- the resurrection of Jesus
- the personal experience of believers.

In this chapter, I'll start with the evidence of design, both in the origin of the universe and in the origin of life. Inevitably it will be a bit sciency, but try to persevere, for it's really, really important to understand why the universe and life as we know it can only be the result of intelligent design. That's the first step towards the truth that it was God who designed and made this amazing world. And why is that important? Because God created it for people like you, and then he made you so that he could love you and have you as his friend forever! You are not a random collection of atoms, but the child of a heavenly Father who wanted to have you in his family even before the world was made. Stay with me while I open your eyes!

The problem with atheism

If I were to tell you that there is no intelligent life in the universe beyond the earth, you'd be right to ask how I could possibly know that for certain. I might *believe* it for some reason, but I could never *know* it by human means unless I first explored every cubic centimetre in the universe and located no trace of intelligent life. Even then I might miss what I was looking for, if there were an

---

[6] For most Jews the second item is not the resurrection of Jesus but their existence as a nation, which can be explained only by God's miraculous dealings with them in their early history.

intelligent life form that didn't consist of physical atoms and molecules detectable by human senses.

Similarly if you were to tell me that there is no God, I'd be in my rights to ask how you could possibly know that for certain. You might *believe* it for some reason—perhaps because your parents taught you not to believe in God, or because of some awful experience you have had, or the ungodly behaviour of people who claim to believe in God, or simply because by believing there is no God you can feel free to choose for yourself how to live and what to believe. You might well find reasons to *believe* there is no God, but I can't see how you can *know* there is no God unless you first explore the entire universe to be sure he isn't hiding somewhere. And even then you might miss what you are looking for, if God doesn't consist of physical atoms and molecules detectable by human senses.

So I can't see how anyone can *know* that there is no God, any more than I can know that there are no other forms of intelligent life in the universe, unless God himself tells me so. And I can't see any rational atheist claiming to know that God doesn't exist because God has told him so!

Actually I find it odd that those who are convinced that other intelligent life forms must exist are often the very people who are convinced that God doesn't exist, even though God by any definition is another intelligent life form. The human mind is very strange at times! Personally, I think it's far easier to believe that God does exist than that he doesn't. For a start there is the evidence of design in the origin of the universe and the origin of life on earth.

The universe

(i) The divine watchmaker

Traditionally, the principal argument for a belief in God's existence is the one given by Paul in chapter 1 of his letter to the Romans in the Bible. He wrote, '*Ever since the creation of the world* [God's] *invisible nature, namely, his eternal power and deity, has been clearly perceived in the things that have been made.*' (Romans 1.20)

The Evidence of Design

In 1802 William Paley expressed the idea more clearly in his argument for a 'divine watchmaker'.[7] Paley said that if one examines the mechanism of a watch, it is obvious that it has been designed to display the time, and if it has been designed then a designer must exist. Similarly, if it is obvious that the universe has been designed, then its designer must exist. But is it obvious that the universe has been designed? Not according to the Big Bang theory.

(ii) The Big Bang theory

Early one January morning, I turned on the light in my office, and one of the three bulbs in the ceiling lamp exploded. There was a flash and a bang, and small pieces of glass and black plastic flew out in all directions around the room. Naturally, they all travelled in straight lines, except for a downward curve due to the force of gravity acting on them. The explosion was frightening, but think how much more frightening it would have been if some of those little particles, instead of heading straight for the walls, had suddenly altered their course and headed for me! It would have meant that some unknown force was controlling their motion, turning them into guided missiles! For nowadays, most of us know the truth of Isaac Newton's first law of motion: 'Every body persists in its state of being at rest or of moving uniformly straight forward, except insofar as it is compelled to change its state by force impressed.'[8]

Just as those particles could not have changed course and headed for me without some external force being 'impressed' upon them, so it would have been equally impossible for them to start playing ring-a-ring o' roses around the ceiling light. Yet in contradiction to Newton's first law of motion and to all that we instinctively know about the way things behave naturally, the Big Bang theory states that the particles which flew outwards after the Big Bang explosion did exactly that—they changed course and many of them started to chase each other round in circles: planets orbiting stars!

---

[7] *Natural Theology or Evidences of the Existence and Attributes of the Deity.* W.Paley, John Morgan, Philadelphia, 1802.

[8] *Lex I: Corpus omne perseverare in statu suo quiescendi vel movendi uniformiter in directum, nisi quatenus a viribus impressis cogitur statum illum mutare.* From *Philosophiæ Naturalis Principia Mathematica.* Sir Isaac Newton, published 5 July 1687.

The Big Bang theory has been widely accepted by scientists for the last 60 years or so as an explanation of the formation of the universe as we know it. It's important to understand that it is only a theory, not a fact as the media usually portray it. It is simply a way to explain how the universe might have been formed if it was not created supernaturally as the Bible tells us it was. The Big Bang theory does not have an explanation for the origin of the matter and energy that existed at the beginning, nor for the existence of time and space, but it does attempt to explain how the physical universe was then able to evolve without further input from a designer or creator.

As I understand it, the theory states that about 13.7 billion years ago all the matter and energy in the universe was concentrated into a single incredibly tiny point. This was not somewhere in space because even space did not exist. For some reason there was a huge explosion, which caused everything, including space, to blow apart in all directions, resulting in a universe that is still expanding today. Within minutes the initial incredibly hot particles combined to form hydrogen and helium atoms through nuclear fusion, and eventually vast quantities of these materials coalesced through gravitational attraction to form stars. Supernova stars generated many of the heavier elements through further nuclear fusion and then exploded, scattering these elements into space where they eventually formed planets orbiting stars like our Sun. I believe that is the general picture even if I haven't got every detail right.

(iii) The laws of physics

One of the three fundamental principles of the Big Bang theory is that the laws of physics are universal and don't change with time or location in space. That has to be a principle, because if a theory is based on the assumption that anything could have happened it ceases to be a scientific theory and becomes mere fanciful conjecture. In his book *Evolution of Earth and its Climate*[9] the Russian professor O.G.Sorokhtin and his colleagues reviewed the current theories about the origins of the Earth and the Moon. They state as a fundamental principle, 'Earth is a physical body and evolves under

---

[9] *Evolution of Earth and its Climate*. O.G.Sorokhtin, G.V.Chilingarian & N.O.Sorokhtin, Elsevier, 2010.

The Evidence of Design

the strict laws of physics.' This means that any naturalistic explanation of the origin of stars, planets and moons must be in keeping with the known physical laws of matter, motion and energy. There can be no escaping them. And that is the very reason I believe that any naturalistic explanation of the formation of the universe is impossible.

Here are some of the strict laws of physics to which Sorokhtin referred:

- Newton's first law of motion states in essence that an object remains at rest or continues to move at a constant speed in a straight line unless some external force acts upon it.
- Newton's law of universal gravitation tells us that the gravitational attraction between two objects diminishes as the distance between them increases, in a fixed way depending on their masses and the distance between them.[10] I don't know whether the same relationship applies to subatomic forces but it seems obvious to me that subatomic forces of mutual attraction will also decrease as the distance between subatomic particles increases.
- Newton's second law of motion,[11] combined with his law of gravitation and some mathematics, tells us how stars, comets, planets, moons and man-made satellites move in relation to each other and the exact courses that they travel on.
- Newton's third law of motion says that if a body A applies some action to a body B then the body B will apply an equivalent action in the opposite direction to body A. Commonly this is stated as 'action and reaction are equal and opposite'.

---

[10] More precisely, the law of universal gravitation states that the gravitational force that two objects exert on each other is equal to Gm_1m_2/r^2, where G is the universal gravitational constant, m_1 and m_2 are the masses of the two objects respectively, and r is the distance between them.

[11] Newton's second law of motion states that $F = m/\alpha$ where F is the force acting on a body of mass m and α is the resulting acceleration in the direction of the force.

- Boyle's law leads to the popular truth that a gas expands to fill the space available. (Fortunately, this is overruled by gravity when a gas is part of the atmosphere around a planet!)

(iv) The Big Bang and the laws of physics

Now let's see what happens when we apply these laws to the current theories about the formation of the universe.

The Big Bang theory states that all the original material of the universe burst out from one infinitesimal point. However it may have emerged (and there are various versions of the theory), it must have emerged in all directions to make a 3-dimensional universe which still appears to be expanding in all directions.[12] According to Newton's first law of motion, all the particles that comprised this material would each have continued travelling in straight lines away from the origin. So it's obvious that any two subatomic particles must either have stuck together and followed the same line of travel or else have moved further and further apart like the spokes of a wheel forever. In that case they would never have come together again, and everything that follows in the Big Bang theory would have been impossible.[13]

Any theory about the origin of the solar system has to explain how the planets ended up travelling around the sun. The current consensus is that at some early point in its evolution the solar system was somewhat like a gigantic spinning plate, bits of which gradually gathered together into planets. This is referred to as the 'solar nebular

---

[12] If it had all emerged in one direction something must have been pushing it that way, and according to the theory there wasn't anything else.

[13] In a homogenous universe, which is the second principal assumption of the Big Bang theory, the distribution of any subatomic forces from adjacent particles would have been equal on all sides and would therefore have cancelled each other out, allowing each particle to continue on its original course in a straight line. Of course, if the force of the Big Bang explosion was insufficient to overcome the total gravitational attraction then all the particles would eventually have been pulled back together into their original point of origin, but then the physical universe as we know it could never have evolved.

disk theory'. As such the system has what is termed an angular momentum, with Jupiter and the outer planets comprising most of this momentum. According to Newton's third law of motion, whatever initially produced this angular momentum must itself have become subject to an equal and opposite angular momentum, and the Big Bang theory offers no explanation of what this other entity might have been.[14] Since the solar system is still rotating, then whatever it was that caused it to rotate—if the cause was natural—is still rotating invisibly in the opposite direction somewhere around us!

And how did the Earth itself start to spin? A cricket ball doesn't spin by itself. To spin a cricket ball the bowler pushes it up on one side with his thumb and pushes it down on the other side with his fingers. Both forces have to be equal and must be applied in opposite directions at the same time. So what possible forces could have been applied simultaneously in opposite directions to spin the Earth, and how could they have been applied to the Earth anyway?

Some scientists suggest that a planet's moons make it rotate, but Venus and Mercury rotate and they don't have moons, while the Earth's moon is doing its best to *stop* the Earth rotating due to tidal braking. The only force that a moon can apply to a planet that doesn't have oceans is towards itself,[15] and a force applied in that direction will not cause a planet to rotate faster or slower.

---

[14] The angular momentum of the solar system could be explained if all the planets had somehow come from outer space into orbit around the Sun in the same direction of rotation and in the same plane, but this would have been impossible for the same reason that the Moon could not have come into orbit around the Earth, which I explain later. In any case, scientists don't generally believe that the planets arrived from outer space. Another explanation for the rotation of planetary systems would be that it is the result of a vortex. A vortex occurs when a liquid or gas is forced down some kind of tube, for example when water drains down a plughole or a column of warm air is drawn up within surrounding colder air to create a tornado. But even in these circumstances the surrounding 'tube' experiences an equal and opposite rotational force on it. And what kind of eternal 'tube' could have surrounded an entire planetary system, and what kind of force (gravity or pressure) could have forced an entire planetary system through the tube to cause it to rotate?

[15] The gravitational attraction between a moon and its planet acts in a direction parallel to the line joining their centres.

How did the Moon come to orbit the Earth? Scientists generally agree that the Moon did not come off the Earth itself, because the mineral compositions of the Earth and the Moon are very different.[16] Most of them believe it originally approached the Earth from space, like some humongous meteor. Newton's second law of motion combined with his law of gravitation and some mathematics tells us exactly what would have happened to this approaching lump of matter. It would either have crashed into the Earth or it would have passed it by. It would never, ever, have ended up in orbit around the Earth by purely natural means. A prospective moon, comet or meteor that was not on an actual collision course with the Earth would approach it along a parabolic path (roughly the shape of a very slack washing line). When it reached its closest point (the lowest point of the washing line) it would depart by a route on the other side of the Earth that was an exact mirror image of its approach path. Any final year high school maths student can tell you that.

In order for the Moon to have come into a permanent orbit around the Earth it would have had to be under some manner of intelligent control, either onboard or remote, and it would have needed inconceivably powerful retrorockets to slow it down at just the right moment, in the same way as rockets are fired remotely on unmanned spaceships to put them into orbit around a planet when they reach it.

Furthermore, to put the Moon into a *circular* orbit around the Earth, these hypothetical onboard rocket brakes would have had to be fired at the exact moment that it was at its nearest point to the Earth, with the exact amount of force necessary to reduce its speed to the required value[17] and in a direction exactly opposite to its direction of travel. It is quite impossible to conceive how such a force could have been applied naturally to slow down the incoming Moon sufficiently, and it is equally impossible to conceive how it could have been applied with the exact strength and direction necessary to put the Moon into the almost perfectly circular orbit it is in today.

---

[16] https://www.space.com/earth-moon-different-compositions-surprise.html

[17] For any moon to be in a circular orbit of radius r around a planet of mass M it must be travelling tangentially at a velocity of exactly $(GM/r)^{0.5}$ where G is the universal gravitational constant.

The Evidence of Design

These arguments apply even more pointedly to a hypothesis published in *Nature Geoscience* in 2017.[18] Perhaps realizing that the traditional theory doesn't work, some Israeli researchers have postulated that the early Earth was hit by a series of objects that somehow produced a ring of debris orbiting the planet. This debris eventually coalesced into about twenty moonlets. (Where did that number come from?) Then, over tens of millions of years (of course!) these eventually combined to form our Moon. But how did the postulated debris knocked off the Earth then get into a circular orbit instead of flying off into space in accordance with Newton's first law of motion? And if it did, how did all the pieces of it end up in orbits with radii close enough for them to coalesce? And how likely is it that they all then coalesced anyway, bearing in mind that the asteroid dust that constitutes Saturn's rings has never coalesced, and neither have Jupiter's 53+ moons? This hypothesis of the Moon's origin seems even more far-fetched than the more traditional one.

(v) The laws of thermodynamics.

If the universe was not created supernaturally as the Bible tells us it was, then the way in which it was created must have been in accordance with the natural laws of physics that all scientists accept. So what do the two laws of thermodynamics have to tell us about the origin of the universe?

The First Law of Thermodynamics states that heat and work are both forms of energy. In its simplest form this law states that in any closed system the total amount of energy remains constant—energy cannot be created or destroyed. However, since Einstein's discovery that matter itself is a form of energy, a more complete statement is that in any closed system the total amount of matter and energy remains constant—the total amount cannot change. This leads to a very interesting conclusion. By definition, the universe is a closed system, for the universe by definition is everything that exists. So if the total amount of matter and energy in the universe cannot change, it cannot be created or destroyed, and therefore the universe must have existed forever.

---

[18] *A multiple-impact origin for the Moon*. R.Rufu, O.Aharonson & H.B.Perets, Nature Geoscience, January 2017.

But then we come to the Second Law of Thermodynamics. This one is harder to explain, but I'll do my best. A really simple way to view it is that the universe is like a gigantic clockwork motor that was once fully wound up but is now running down.

Above the town of Llanberis in North Wales there is what is known as the Electric Mountain. During the day, water from a reservoir at the top of the mountain flows downhill into another reservoir and on the way down it drives a turbine that generates electricity for the national grid. During the night, when the demand for electricity from the grid is reduced and there is plenty to spare, an electric motor powered from the grid pumps the water at the bottom back up the mountain.

But suppose this were a closed system, unconnected to the grid, and with no rainfall to top up the mountainside reservoir. During the day the water would drive the turbine which would then store the generated electricity in some kind of gigantic rechargeable battery. During the night the electricity stored in the battery would be used to pump the water back up the mountain. You might imagine that this could continue forever, but the Second Law of Thermodynamics says that the amount of water that could be pumped back up the mountain would always be less than the amount that came down the previous night. Eventually the whole system would run down and come to a stop, with all the water in the bottom reservoir and no power left in the battery.

The reason this would happen is not that the energy in the system would somehow evaporate, but that the useful energy which was initially stored in the upper reservoir would turn into useless energy in the form of heat. Electric motors generate heat: so do batteries when they are being charged. The Second Law states that while the total amount of energy in the universe remains constant, the amount of useful energy is constantly decreasing, until eventually there will be none left, and any kind of work will be impossible.

And once again this leads to a surprising conclusion. Since the amount of useful energy is continually decreasing, the universe cannot have been running down forever, for if it had then by now there would be no useful energy left. Therefore the universe cannot have existed forever, which means *it must have had a beginning in time.*

So the First Law of Thermodynamics tells us that the universe must have existed forever, while the Second Law of

The Evidence of Design

Thermodynamics tells us that it cannot have existed forever.[19] Obviously something is wrong, and what is wrong is this. It is the idea that the universe came into existence naturally in accordance with all the natural laws of physics, rather than by the supernatural, awe-inspiring, inconceivably powerful word of the living God.

By faith we understand that the world was created by the word of God, so that what is seen was made out of things which do not appear.
                                                                Hebrews 11.3

(vi) A statistical argument

Finally I have my own statistical argument against the idea that the solar system could have come into existence without some supernatural design and control.

At the time of writing, 293 moons have been identified in the solar system.[20] Let's assume the impossible—that somehow all these moons did get captured naturally without some kind of control system to put them into orbit. In that case, it is exceedingly likely that most or all of the resulting orbits would be ellipses, i.e. squashed circles. The amount that a circle is squashed is called its eccentricity. A perfect circle has an eccentricity of 0.0 and a totally squashed circle has an eccentricity of 1.0. The oval shape of a hen's egg for example has an eccentricity of about 0.7. The orbit of Halley's comet around the Sun has an eccentricity of 0.967: it is extremely long and thin. The Moon's orbit, on the other hand, has an eccentricity of only 0.0554. This means that it is an almost perfect circle, for in an orbit with an eccentricity of 0.05 the narrowest part still measures 99.9% of the widest part.

Now an orbit created at random by a moon approaching a planet and *somehow* being captured by it, could have an eccentricity of

---

[19] Physicists are fully aware of this anomaly. Some of them try to get round it via quantum mechanics, because experiments in quantum mechanics appear to show that individual particles can 'pop' in and out of existence. But even if that were true, it wouldn't begin to prove that an entire universe can pop into existence. I can lift a feather, but that hardly proves I can lift a mountain. And how could space and time have 'popped' into existence? Not even quantum mechanics has an answer to that.
[20] http://ssd.jpl.nasa.gov/sats/elem. Viewed April 2024.

God, Science and the Bible

anything from 0.0 to almost 1.0. We would therefore expect an orbit as precisely circular as our own moon's to be extremely rare. So it is surprising that the orbits of 64 of the solar system's 293 known moons have an eccentricity of 0.05 or less, meaning that all their orbits are almost perfectly circular.[21]

It is possible to calculate the probability of this happening by chance.[22] If we assume that the probability of a randomly elliptical orbit having an eccentricity of less than 0.05 is 1 in 20 (i.e. 1/0.05), then the chance that at least 64 of the 293 moons will have orbits with eccentricities of less than 0.05 by accident is 1 in 6.6×10^{22}. 6.6×10^{22} is a very large number. It is 6.6 thousand billion billion, and that is over 300 times as many stars as there are in the entire observable universe![23] *In other words having 64 out of 293 moons in nearly circular orbits around their planets merely by chance is as likely as picking the winning lottery ball out of the same number of lottery balls as there are stars in 300 universes!*

This makes complete nonsense of the idea that if there were a large enough number of planetary systems in the universe then at least one of them would have to be like ours. There aren't enough stars to make this even remotely possible. And even if there were, I cannot conceive how even one single moon could have ended up in any kind of orbit round its planet, whether in a circle or an ellipse, if it had to arrive there in accordance with 'the strict laws of physics' as Sorokhtin demanded.

Incidentally, 2649 other planetary systems have been detected at the time of writing, but according to a paper by Marcy and others[24], '*the solar system, with its unusually low eccentricity, is rare and unique.*'

It is precisely because I believe in the fundamental laws of physics that I cannot believe the universe was formed naturally. It can only have been created by a supernatural God. Sir Isaac Newton came to exactly the same conclusion: '*This most beautiful system of the*

---

[21] The eccentricities of the Solar System's moon orbits are listed by NASA on their website http://ssd.jpl.nasa.gov/sats/elem. Viewed April 2024.
[22] The calculation can be downloaded from www.booksforlife.today/files/circular-orbit-probabilities.xls.
[23] https://www.space.com/26078-how-many-stars-are-there.html
[24] *Orbital Eccentricities*. G.Marcy and others, http://exoplanets.org. Viewed June 2023.

sun, planets and comets could proceed only from the counsel and dominion of an intelligent and powerful Being.'[25]

Today the progress of physicists and mathematicians to produce a 'theory of everything' is increasing mankind's understanding of the awesome nature of the universe as it now is. But even the Big Bang theory does not attempt to explain the origin of the universe—where all the original matter and energy came from. More importantly, no one—not even the late Professor Stephen Hawking—could ever disprove the Bible's declaration that the universe was created supernaturally. For even if the universe was created supernaturally yesterday we would never know it, as we shall see in Chapter 5.

Life

(i) The origin of species

If neither the universe as a whole nor life on Earth was created by some powerful and intelligent entity, where does that leave us? Taking a step back from the picture we can only conclude that somehow hydrogen turned into people all by itself. Whole books have been written explaining how this could or could not have happened, so I can't pretend to do the subject justice in a book that has a more modest but infinitely more important goal: that of helping you to believe in God as Creator and in his Son Jesus as the promised Saviour and King to come. However I do want to suggest a few thoughts that I have had about the origin of species. To my mind these thoughts point once again to the existence of a God who brought everything into existence on purpose.

The title of Charles Darwin's 1859 book *On the Origin of Species by Means of Natural Selection, or the Preservation of Favoured Races in the Struggle for Life* was a little misleading. Darwin did not try to explain how life itself (the ability to engage with the environment and reproduce) originated.[26] He simply proposed that all living species

---

[25] Philosophiæ Naturalis Principia Mathematica. Sir Isaac Newton, published 5 July 1687.
[26] When asked how life began, atheist Professor Richard Dawkins, author of *The God Delusion*, responded, "Nobody knows how it got started." But this was untrue: God has told us.

God, Science and the Bible

had arisen from some simple original life form through the natural selection of small, random, inherited variations that increased each individual's ability to compete, survive, and reproduce. Over a very long period, these small changes led to large changes and eventually to the plants, insects, fish, reptiles, animals, birds and people that we see today.

Note the phrase, 'natural selection'. Natural selection is the process by which certain *existing* traits in a living organism become more or less common in succeeding generations due to environmental factors that favour or inhibit the organism's ability to produce surviving offspring. It does not involve the creation of anything new, which is an essential requirement for the origin of new species!

(ii) Natural selection

In the 1970s, a prominent evolutionist, Dr. John Endler, carried out some clever research on the colourful guppy fish. He had the idea that the most colourful males would be more successful in attracting females and hence produce more offspring, but that the less colourful ones would find it easier to hide from predators and so would survive longer. By separating them into three different ponds, one with natural predators that preyed on guppies, one with predatory fish that didn't prey on guppies, and the third with no natural predators, he was able to show that over several generations the offspring in the first pond containing guppy predators were indeed less colourful and had fewer spots than the guppies in the other two ponds. But they were still guppies.

Similarly, it has been claimed that during the Industrial Revolution in Great Britain, peppered moths in cities became much darker, almost black. Previously the moths had been speckled, but they were mostly fairly light in colour, their colouration camouflaging them against the tree trunks that some of them rested on during the daytime, thereby protecting them from predatory birds. Nevertheless their colours varied: some were lighter and some were darker than others. On smoke-blackened city trees, the darker ones were less easily distinguishable, with the result that within 50 years most of the peppered moths in cities had become very dark in colour.[27] But whatever the truth of this story, they were still peppered moths.[28]

Those are two examples of natural selection. But evolution demands more than natural selection. It requires organisms to do more than separate into groups with characteristics that are more or less favourable for particular environments. By positing a common ancestry for all living things, evolution requires the production by stages of radically *new* traits that are not just selections from existing ones or even minor modifications of them. The theory requires a simpler kind of life form to change into a more complex kind, so that one basic type, i.e. one kind of plant, insect or animal, etc., eventually changes into another, more complex one.

The problem is that people who support the theory of evolution continually tout instances of natural selection as though they were instances of evolution. For example, Wendy Prosser describes three instances of changes 'demonstrating natural selection' and then she calls them 'evolution in action'.[29] Sewall Wright described the case of the peppered moth as 'the clearest case in which a conspicuous evolutionary process has actually been observed',[30] yet no new kinds of moth were formed! Professor Richard Dawkins described Endler's experiment with guppies as 'a spectacular example of evolution before our very eyes'[31] but it was nothing of the sort. Endler himself wrote, '*Natural selection must not be equated with evolution, though the two are*

---

[27] See http://creation.com/more-about-moths for the full story of the peppered moth saga. Viewed June 2023.

[28] L.Harrison Matthews wrote in the foreword to the 1971 edition of Darwin's *Origin of Species*, 'The experiments beautifully demonstrate natural selection—or survival of the fittest—in action, but they do not show evolution in progress, for however the populations may alter in their content of light, intermediate or dark forms, all the moths remain from beginning to end *Biston betularia*.'

[29] http://www.decodedscience.org/evolution-in-action-three-experiments-demonstrating-natural-selection/1796. Viewed 12 September 2016, but now unavailable..

[30] *Encyclopedia of Evolution*. S.A.Rice, New York: Facts On File, Inc. p.308.

[31] *The Greatest Show on Earth*. R.Dawkins, Free Press, New York, 2009. p.139.

intimately related.'³² And in the same book Endler added, '*Natural selection does not explain the origin of new variants, only the process of changes in their frequency.*'³³

So if examples of mere natural selection are the clearest evidence of 'evolution in action' that its supporters can cite, one can only conclude that actual examples of evolution taking place are non-existent. There are certainly fossils of life forms that no longer exist, but that doesn't prove that they must have changed into something else. All they tell us is that there were once some life forms like the dodo that are now extinct. There is absolutely no fossil evidence of one species gradually turning into another. If anything, the evidence from fossils *disproves* the theory evolution. Let's be clear about this. There is no scientific, observable evidence in support of evolution as an explanation for the origin of species. The evolutionary hypothesis is simply an idea, an idea that particularly appeals to people who don't want to believe that everything was designed and created by God.

(iii) Mutations

It is true that *mutations* occur. A mutation is a change in the DNA sequence in a gene. A mutated gene is like the letters of 'semolina' rearranged to read 'is no meal'. It is like Eric Morecambe's famous attempt at a piano solo, when he played 'all the right notes but not necessarily in the right order'. What is the result of such mutations? The most obvious example is ageing. Apart from our brain cells and eye lenses, the cells in our bodies are continually being replaced, some frequently like our hair and blood, some less frequently like our fat cells and bones. But around the age of 25 or 30 genetic mutations begin to become significant. The replacement process begins to go wrong: our replacement hair is thinner, our new skin is wrinkled and our joints begin to creak. Another example of mutation is the creation of damaged genes at conception, resulting in offspring with physical or mental disabilities.

---

[32] *Natural Selection in the Wild.* J.A.Endler, Princeton University Press, NJ, USA, 1986. p.5.
[33] J.A.Endler, as above, p.245.

Some mutations by design can be useful, as the producers of genetically modified crops claim. But even beneficial mutations involve only the suppression, alteration or combination of existing genetic instructions, not the addition of new, more complex ones. Naturally occurring beneficial mutations always involve the loss of some ability rather than the creation of a new one: the loss of sight in cave fish and cave salamanders, the loss of functional wings in beetles on a windy island, the loss of body armour when saltwater stickleback fish are introduced to less dangerous freshwater environments, and so on. These are mutations, but they are not examples of anything new being created, of creatures of one kind evolving into a more complex kind. All they involve is the loss or modification of something that they once possessed.

In human beings, mutations are almost invariably harmful—one database listed 2665 genes with mutations known to cause disease.[34] Fortunately inherited mutations are often eliminated naturally. My mother's second toe on each foot crossed over her big toe but my father's toes were normal. Consequently my second toe is slightly twisted, and my children's toes are fine. It appears that the necessity of mating with another member of the same kind is designed to prevent permanent evolutionary change taking place rather than promote it. And this applies equally to beneficial mutations, so there is no guarantee that even a beneficial one would be preserved in a subsequent generation.

For the theory of evolution to work, mutations have to provide a distinct benefit for survival or reproduction; the benefit has to be sufficiently substantial to ensure that the mutated version of an organism survives better than the non-mutated ones; and the mutation has to be reproduced in successive generations. Since most beneficial mutations appear to be recessive, the latter requirement generally means that in higher life forms the same mutation has to occur in both a male and a female within the same generation who then mate with each other, an occurrence that seems most unlikely.

With all that in mind, a little common sense should convince any rational and unbiased person that the theory of evolution as an

---

[34] *Online Mendelian Inheritance in Man*, omim.org, cited by Dr. Don Batten in *Evolution's Achilles Heels*, R. Carter ed, Creation Book Publishers, Georgia USA, 2014.

explanation of the origin of life's diversity is a non-starter. From Darwin onwards the theory of evolution assumes that genetic mutations occur in small steps, because it is stretching reason too far to believe, for example, that a fully formed and functioning heart could suddenly appear in the genetic code by accident. And for evolution to progress, it is assumed that advantageous mutations will survive while disadvantageous ones will not survive, as a result of natural selection. Taken together, these assumptions mean that each small step must in itself provide some advantage for survival or reproduction that is significant enough for natural selection to pick it up and get it established. And only a little thought demonstrates that that is impossible. Let's take the human bladder as an example.

(iv) A meditation on bladders

Amoebae don't have bladders. Therefore at some point in the supposed evolutionary ancestry of man there was a creature that did not possess a bladder to store waste fluids. Now a bladder can provide an advantage to existence only when it is functional. This means that in order to become established, it must have been sufficiently formed to function when it first appeared.

In order to be functional, it must also have had nerves travelling all the way to the brain capable of telling the brain when it was full, otherwise it would have burst, and bladders that kept bursting would have been a disadvantage to existence rather than an advantage.[35] Those nerves must have developed at the same time as the fully formed bladder did, otherwise they would have served no purpose and would therefore have conferred no evolutionary advantage. At the same time that the nerves were created, an area of the brain that could interpret the meaning of the messages they sent to it must have come into existence, otherwise neither the nerves nor the bladder would have been able to function properly. And at the same time as that, the brain must also have somehow simultaneously acquired by random mutation the means of communicating back to the bladder

---

[35] Sensations from the bladder are transmitted to the central nervous system (CNS) via general visceral afferent fibres (GVA). GVA fibres on the superior surface follow the course of the sympathetic efferent nerves back to the CNS, while GVA fibres on the inferior portion of the bladder follow the course of the parasympathetic efferents.

The Evidence of Design

an instruction to empty itself when it was told that it was full, or it would have burst. *All these amazing random genetic changes must have happened simultaneously for any preferential survival rate to have been produced in any of them.*

But let's suppose that a fully functioning bladder did come into existence through some totally miraculous random mutation. Not only must a bladder be fully formed and functional to be of any use, with all the correct connections to the brain and the required new section of the brain to control it, but it must also come into existence in the right part of the body, joined to an outlet from the kidneys and with its own outlet to the outside world.

Even supposing that a random genetic mutation could somehow produce a fully formed bladder with functional connections to and from the brain, it would not have been helpful if it had appeared around someone's ear, or on someone's little toe, or as an extension to the heart. You may protest that I am unjustifiably ridiculing the idea of evolution, but if genetic mutations producing new information really do occur without some external design and control, then by definition they must occur at random. This means that the first functioning bladder could have occurred at any random point on the body. Can you or anyone else seriously believe that fully functioning bladders appeared at dozens of random positions on the bodies of some ancestral creatures before one happened to appear in the best position to take precedence over all the other ones through natural selection?

Furthermore, what are the chances that a baby born with this miraculous fully formed bladder in the right place and with a modified nervous system and brain to accompany it would grow up and mate with someone who had a similar miraculously formed bladder in the right place at the same time so that they could pass such a genetic deviation on to their children? Especially since male and female bladders are different and are located in different places? A mutated man could not pass his bladder-making instructions to his daughter, nor could a mutated woman pass them on to her son.

It is easier to believe that God made the world in six days than that bladders could have come into existence by chance!

I can't resist quoting this hard-hitting passage from the New Testament:

29

Ever since the creation of the world, [God's] *invisible nature, namely his eternal power and deity, has been clearly perceived in the things that have been made. So they are without excuse; for although they knew God, they did not honour him as God or give thanks to him, but became futile in their thinking and their senseless minds were darkened.*

Romans 1:20-23

(v) Small mutations are not advantageous to survival

A similar argument would apply to almost every member of every creature's body. A bird's feathers give it an added chance of surviving predators only when they have become functional so that it can fly. Intermediate steps towards the development of feathers give a pre-bird no survival advantage and actually reduce its chance of escaping a predator by adding useless weight to it or by disadvantaging otherwise functional forelimbs.

Such considerations expose the Achilles heel in Darwin's theory that life as we know it developed as a result of the 'natural selection of small, random, inherited variations that increased each individual's ability to compete, survive, and reproduce'. Small, random, inherited variations may help with something that already exists like the length of a foot, but small, random variations in the direction of some new organ or ability can never increase an individual's ability to compete, survive and reproduce until the new organ or ability is sufficiently formed and functional. If anything they will hinder a creature's chances of survival and continuity. Therefore, except possibly in the case of improvements to existing organs, small random variations that increase an individual's ability to compete, survive and reproduce will simply never occur. And if the small intermediate steps never occur, then the eventual development of a new functioning organ to which they would otherwise be heading will never occur either.

J.B.S.Haldane, a believer in evolution, calculated that for a new trait or variation to become established, individuals possessing it would have to produce at least 10% more offspring than those who did not possess it, as a result of the advantages it provided.[36] Since small new variations that are only a step on the way to producing

---

[36] The *cost of natural selection*. J.B.S.Haldane, Journal of Genetics 55, pages 511-534, 1957.

The Evidence of Design

something useful provide no advantage at all, by Haldane's calculations they will not become established and will simply disappear in subsequent generations.

Besides all that, as I illustrated in my bladder analogy, every physical ability depends for its functionality on a complex web of nerves, brain processing and the production of specialized hormones, enzymes and other things. Therefore, no new organ or functionality can ever arise at random unless a whole range of random changes occur simultaneously, all of them individually giving no immediate advantage to the creature's chances of survival or reproduction, until one day they all reach completion and suddenly start to function in mutual cooperation as though they had been made for each other. How likely is that?

(vi) The theory of evolution is not a fact: it is a religion

Professor Wolfgang Smith, a mathematician and philosopher who does not believe that God created all the original kinds, nevertheless wrote,

> *I am convinced, moreover, that Darwinism (in whatever form) is not in fact a scientific theory, but a pseudo-metaphysical hypothesis decked out in scientific garb. In reality the theory derives its support not from empirical data or logical deductions of a scientific kind but from the circumstance that it happens to be the only doctrine of biological origins that can be conceived within the constricted Weltanschauung* [world view] *to which a majority of scientists no doubt subscribe.*[37]

Ben Goldacre, whose excellent book *Bad Science* suggests to me that Ben may not even believe in God, wrote this definition of 'communal reinforcement':

> *Communal reinforcement is the process by which a claim becomes a strong belief, through repeated assertion by members of a community. The process is independent of whether the claim has been properly researched, or is*

---

[37] *The Universe is Ultimately to be Explained in Terms of a Metacosmic Reality.* J.W.Smith, Chapter 23 of 'Cosmos, Bios, Theos', ed. H.Margenau & R.A.Varghese, Open Court Publishing Company, December 1991.

> supported by empirical data significant enough to warrant belief by reasonable people.³⁸

He was actually referring to religion, but his words are peculiarly apposite to the theory of evolution. Some of evolution's devotees regard it with almost religious fervour. Think how frequently the idea of evolution is reinforced by the media's continuously mentioning it as though it were a fact, even though it is merely a hypothesis and no one has ever observed anything evolving into something new. Think how evolution is taught as a fact in schools, and how teaching creation as a possible alternative explanation of life is frowned upon or even forbidden. Think how angry and even insulting some of evolutionism's principal proponents become when their views are publicly challenged. Does that suggest that they are unprejudiced scientists seeking to discover the truth, or does it rather suggest that they are ardent devotees to a religious faith, who cannot face any attack on it, however rationally it is presented?

In 1997, Dr Richard Lewontin wrote, 'Our willingness to accept scientific claims that are against common sense is the key to an understanding of the real struggle between science and the supernatural. We take the side of science, *in spite of the patented absurdity of some of its constructs*... because we have a prior commitment, a commitment to materialism... Moreover, that materialism is absolute, for we cannot allow a Divine Foot in the door."³⁹

So much for 'unbiased scientists'!

(vii) The origin of life: conclusion

Even if I didn't believe in anything supernatural, my faith could never stretch to believe in the theory of evolution as stated by Darwin and his successors. At its heart there is the insurmountable self-contradiction that the required small random changes on the road to something better cannot in themselves provide any evolutionary advantage and will therefore not persist through natural selection. The unimaginably complex and interacting systems that comprise any

---

[38] *Bad Science*. B.Goldacre, Fourth Estate, London, 2009.
[39] The New York Review, page 31, 9 January 1997. My italics. Actually, God made the door!

functional living organ could not have evolved in the random manner that Darwin proposed: they can only be the result of design. And if there is design, there is a designer. Therefore the most rational and likely explanation for our existence is that there *is* a God who designed and created you and me, and every other life form 'according to their kinds', just as the Bible declares.

> *God created the great sea monsters and every living creature that moves, with which the waters swarm, according to their kinds, and every winged bird according to its kind. ...the beasts of the earth according to their kinds and the cattle according to their kinds, and everything that creeps upon the ground according to its kind. And God saw that it was good.*
> Genesis 1.21,25

> *The Lord God formed man of dust from the ground, and breathed into his nostrils the breath of life; and man became a living being.*
> Genesis 2.7

> *For thou didst form my inward parts, thou didst knit me together in my mother's womb... Wonderful are thy works!*
> Psalm 139.13,14

God, Science and the Bible

3. The Evidence of the Resurrection

Contemporary writers

In searching for evidence of God's existence we now leave the realms of science and turn to history.

Someone once claimed that Shakespeare's plays were not written by William Shakespeare but by a completely unknown person of the same name! This strange statement highlights one truth: whoever it was who wrote the plays, somebody did, otherwise they would not exist. Similarly someone was responsible for the revolutionary and powerfully memorable teaching that has been recorded as the teaching of Jesus of Nazareth, and it would be extremely strange if it were anyone other than Jesus, the Galilean carpenter. Actually there is more historical evidence that Jesus existed than Julius Caesar did, for within 60 years of Jesus's death at least four biographies of his life had been written, as well as twenty-one letters referring to him. Furthermore, in museums and libraries around the world today there are ancient copies of manuscripts dated to within 150 years or so of his death, written by dozens of people who all referred to Jesus and his life, teaching, death or resurrection.[40]

The Jewish historian Josephus, writing his *Antiquities of the Jews* in AD 93 or 94, mentioned the death about 70 years earlier of Jesus's contemporary, John the Baptist. He also mentioned the stoning to death of the second Christian martyr, James, by order of Ananus ben Ananus, a Herodian high priest, in AD 44. Josephus described James as 'the brother of Jesus, who was called Christ'. In all known versions of the *Antiquities*, Josephus included the following passage:

---

[40] There was a first century manual for new Christians entitled the Didache (the Teaching), and early references to Jesus in the writings of Clemens Romanus, a bishop of Rome who died in AD 99. Some of the so-called early church fathers who wrote about Jesus in the second century were Irenaeus, Justinius, Marcion, Papias, Tatiani Diatessaron and Valentinani.

God, Science and the Bible

> *Now there was about this time* [when the Jews of Judea were governed by the Roman procurator Pontius Pilate] *Jesus, a wise man, if it be lawful to call him a man, for he was a doer of wonderful works, a teacher of such men as receive the truth with pleasure. He drew over to him many of the Jews and many of the Gentiles. He was the Christ. When Pilate, at the suggestion of the principal men among us, had condemned him to the cross, those that loved him at the first did not forsake him; for he appeared to them alive again the third day; as the divine prophets had foretold these and ten thousand other wonderful things concerning him. And the tribe of Christians so named from him are not extinct at this day.*[41]

Most scholars believe that Josephus did originally write this passage about the life and death of Jesus, but that some parts were inserted later by Christians when they made copies of it. The parts that speak about the life and death of Jesus and the belief of his first followers in his resurrection are considered genuine.[42]

In about AD 112, the Roman emperor Trajan sent a man named Pliny to reorganize the affairs of the province of Bithynia. Bithynia was in modern Turkey. Pliny wrote to Trajan asking for his advice on how to deal with the Christians he found there, 'for the contagion of that superstition has penetrated not the cities only, but the villages and country'. He wrote of almost deserted Roman temples, and very few buyers of animals to sacrifice in them. Clearly, within 80 years of Christ's death, multitudes of people believed what Pliny called 'a perverse and extravagant superstition', namely that Jesus had risen from the dead.

---

[41] *Antiquities of the Jews*, F.Josephus, 18.3.3 §63.

[42] My guess at Josephus's original version would be this: '*Now there was about this time Jesus, a wise man, a doer of wonderful works, a teacher of such men as receive the truth with pleasure. He drew over to him many of the Jews and many of the Gentiles, who believed he was the Christ. When Pilate, at the suggestion of the principal men among us, had condemned him to the cross, those that loved him at the first did not forsake him; for he appeared to them alive again the third day. And the tribe of Christians so named from him are not extinct at this day.*' (I think the sentence about returning to life on the third day was written by Josephus, for it explains the surprising fact that the Christians continued to believe he was the Messiah even after he had been crucified.)

The Evidence of the Resurrection

Five years after Pliny wrote to Trajan, a Greek author, Lucian of Samosata was born. He came to be known as 'the Atheist' because he made fun of both philosophy and religion. (He is credited with writing the world's first science fiction story, although the fiction in it vastly outdid the science. Entitled *The True History* it was a satire on Homer's *Odyssey* and described a journey to the moon and back.) In his biography of Peregrinus, Lucian wrote factually about Christians:

> *They still worship that great man, the fellow who was crucified in Palestine for bringing this new cult into the world... the poor souls have persuaded themselves that they are immortal and will live forever. As a result, they think nothing of death, and most of them are perfectly willing to sacrifice themselves. Besides, their first law-giver has convinced them that once they stop believing in Greek gods and start worshipping that crucified sage of theirs and live according to his laws, they are all each other's brothers and sisters. So taking this information on trust, without any guarantee of its truth, they believe in common ownership, which means that any unscrupulous adventurer who comes along can soon make a fortune out of them.*[43]

In AD 64 a great fire destroyed most of Rome. It was generally believed that the emperor, Nero, had instigated it in order to rebuild the city to his own design. In order to divert the blame he fastened it on Christians, who had been predicting that the world would end in fire (2 Peter 3.10) and that Rome in particular would be burned (Revelation 18.8-10; 19.3). Fifty years after the fire the Roman historian Tacitus described what happened:[44]

> *To get rid of the report, Nero fastened the guilt and inflicted the most exquisite tortures on a class hated for their abominations, called Christians by the populace. Christus, from whom the name had its origin, suffered the extreme penalty during the reign of Tiberius at the hands of one of our procurators, Pontius Pilatus... Accordingly an arrest was first made of all who confessed; then, upon their information, an immense multitude was convicted, not so much of the crime of arson, as of hatred of*

---

[43] Quoted in *Lucian: Satirical Sketches*. Translated by P.Turner, The Penguin Classics, Penguin Books, 1961, p.11.

[44] *Annals*. Tacitus, XV.44.2-8.

> *the human race... Covered with the skins of beasts, they were torn by dogs and perished, or were nailed to crosses, or were doomed to the flames...*

So within only 45 years of Christ's death, there was already 'an immense multitude' of Christians nearly a thousand miles away in Rome! Something equivalent to a historical nuclear bomb must have exploded to cause so many people to believe so firmly that Jesus Christ had conquered death that they were willing to lose their lives rather than deny it.

These extracts are just part of the mass of historical evidence for the existence of Jesus as a teacher in Palestine who was crucified yet nevertheless founded a mass movement of people who believed that he had then returned from the dead. Whatever could have persuaded so many people to believe this, even at the risk of arrest and death, if it didn't actually happen?

The Bible's account

Let's begin by reviewing some of the key events in the original story, as reported by four of Jesus's own followers, Matthew, Mark, Luke and John. These men were responsible for writing the 'Gospels', the first four books in the second part of the Bible, the part that is known as the New Testament. The four Gospels tell the story of Jesus's life and teaching.

Matthew and John were two of Jesus's twelve 'disciples', men who left their jobs to be with Jesus throughout the two years of his teaching ministry.

Mark was the son in a family that helped to support Jesus. He became a close friend of Jesus's chief disciple, Peter, from whom he got much of his information. Peter himself wrote two letters that are in the New Testament.

Luke was an educated doctor and historian who had followed the events concerning Jesus's life and ministry from early on and decided to put into writing what he had learned. His sources appear to have included Mary, the mother of Jesus. (Luke 1.1-4)

Paul. While I'm doing introductions, I must mention Paul. Paul (or Sha'ul as he was originally called) was a devout Jewish scholar. He didn't originally believe that Jesus was the promised Jewish Messiah nor that he had risen from the dead, so he actually organized the arrest and death of some of the first believers for telling people that Jesus was the Son of God. But then Jesus miraculously appeared to Paul in a manner so convincing that Paul became the first missionary to the non-Jewish world. (Acts 9.15) Paul wrote some important letters to churches he founded, several of which form part of the New Testament and include teaching about Christ's coming return.

In the Gospels, some details of the four accounts of Jesus's death and resurrection differ, as is often the case with witnesses to real events, but on all the main points they agree.

The Jewish leaders in Jerusalem decided that Jesus must die. In some of his preaching, Jesus had seemed to be claiming equality with God, and people were believing him. Aside from their outrage at this, the Jewish authorities feared he might spearhead a popular uprising against the ruling Romans, which they knew would have ended in disaster.

So late one Thursday evening, after Jesus and his disciples had eaten a last supper together and darkness had come, the priests had him arrested. They conducted a 'trial' during the night. The high priest demanded, *"...tell us if you are the Christ,*[45] *the Son of God."* Jesus replied, *"...you will see the Son of man seated at the right hand of Power, and coming on the clouds of heaven,"* clearly referring to himself. (Matthew 26.63,64)[46] The high priest interpreted this as blasphemy, which in Jewish law carried the death penalty.

But the Jewish leaders were not permitted by Roman law to put anyone to death. So early next morning they woke up the Roman procurator, Pontius Pilate, and told him that Jesus had been stirring up a rebellion. After a somewhat inconclusive cross-examination Pilate was persuaded by the riotous shouting of the high priest's rent-

---

[45] 'The Christ' or 'the Messiah' meant literally 'the anointed' or 'chosen one'. Based on prophecies in the Old Testament, the Jews had believed for generations that one day God would send an anointed deliverer to set their nation free and set up a kingdom of righteousness.

[46] Jesus was actually referring to a passage in chapter 7 of the Old Testament book of Daniel, in which Daniel had a vision of a 'son of man' in the clouds of heaven being given authority by God to rule over all the nations for eternity. The Jewish rulers would have understood perfectly that Jesus was claiming to be this person.

God, Science and the Bible

a-mob outside his palace to hand Jesus over to be crucified, the standard Roman punishment at that time for serious criminals.

After being flogged to the point of exhaustion, Jesus was taken to be crucified, in company with two other criminals. The crucifixion was very public with numerous witnesses, and it was supervised by a Roman centurion who was assisted by several soldiers.

Jesus's body was attached to a wooden cross by large nails that the soldiers drove through his hands.[47] He prayed, *"Father, forgive them, for they know not what they do."* (Luke 23.34)

Around 3:00 p.m. the Jewish leaders asked Pilate to order the criminals' legs to be broken in order to finish them off, so that their dead bodies could be taken away. This was because at sundown a Jewish sabbath would begin, and it was a very special one when they would celebrate their forefathers' escape from Egypt. They didn't want it to be spoilt by the sight of dead bodies hanging around. Pilate agreed, but when the soldiers found that Jesus was already dead one of them stuck a spear in his side instead of breaking his legs. The disciple, John, who was watching, saw blood and water flow out of Jesus's side.

In the evening two sympathizers, a wealthy man named Joseph and a Jewish leader named Nicodemus, teamed up and obtained Pilate's permission to bury Jesus's body. They wrapped it in linen cloths and laid it in a cave that Joseph had previously hewn out of the rock in his garden, presumably for the purpose of family burials. John tells us that they used 100 pounds' weight of spices to embalm the body, but the other three writers seem to contradict this.[48]

---

[47] It is not certain whether the nails went through Jesus's hands or wrists, nor how the rest of his body was supported.

[48] According to John's account, Joseph and Nicodemus first bound the body with linen cloths and about a hundred pounds' weight of myrrh and aloes, effectively mummifying the body. According to Matthew's and Luke's accounts Joseph simply wrapped it in a clean linen shroud and laid it in his cave while at least two of the women watched him. Luke tells us that they then went and prepared spices and ointments before the Sabbath started at sunset, and Mark and Luke tell us that they turned up first thing on the following Sunday morning when the Sabbath was past with their spices to anoint the body, which all suggest that this had not yet been done. So either the women wanted to add their own spices as a personal tribute to their master, or else the two

The Evidence of the Resurrection

The cave was closed, for security and hygiene, by means of a stone like a giant millstone that had probably been shaped on purpose to roll across the entrance. It was too heavy for three women to move later.

The next day was Saturday, the sabbath rest day. Nevertheless first thing in the morning the Jewish rulers went to Pilate and asked him to arrange for the tomb to be guarded. *"Sir,"* they said, *"we remember how that impostor said, while he was still alive, 'After three days I will rise again.' Therefore order the sepulchre to be made secure until the third day, lest his disciples go and steal him away, and tell the people, 'He has risen from the dead'."* (Matthew 27.63,64) Pilate agreed. He appointed an initial watch of soldiers to seal the stone so that it would be known if anyone subsequently opened it. Since the soldiers were responsible to Pilate for ensuring that the body was not stolen, it is certain that they would first have checked it was still inside! They then stationed themselves on guard.

Around dawn on the Sunday morning, when the day of rest was over, three of the women who were among Jesus's followers and had witnessed both his crucifixion and the place of his burial turned up with their own spices. They were discussing what to do about the stone, when to their amazement they found that it had been rolled aside already. There was no sign of the soldiers, and the cave was empty. They went and told Jesus's male disciples that Jesus's body had gone, but the men didn't believe them.

However John tells us that he[49] and Peter ran to the tomb, looked inside and saw only the grave clothes in two neat piles: the shroud and a separate head-wrapping cloth.

Mary Magdalene returned alone to the tomb and in a moving scene met Jesus alive in the garden. She reported to the disciples that she had 'seen the Lord.'.. They didn't believe that either.

Meanwhile some of the soldiers reported to the chief priests what had happened. The soldiers accepted a bribe to spread the story that

---

men did have the spices as stated but did not actually have time to prepare and make use of them before the Sabbath started. There is clearly some discrepancy between the various accounts.

[49] John is not identified by name, but is referred to as 'the other disciple, the one whom Jesus loved.' Scholars generally take that to mean John himself.

God, Science and the Bible

they had fallen asleep and that Jesus's followers had taken the opportunity to steal the body.

That afternoon, two unnamed disciples were walking to a nearby village when Jesus joined them on the road, but they did not immediately recognize him. When they told him how sad they were that their hopes of a national saviour had been dashed by Jesus's death, he rebuked them for their unbelief. '*...he interpreted to them in all the scriptures the things concerning himself*' (Luke 24.27), explaining how the Messiah's death had been predicted as necessary in the Old Testament. They persuaded him to join them for a meal and stay the night with them. As he gave thanks to God for their food, they suddenly realized who he was, and he immediately vanished. They hastened back to Jerusalem in the darkness to tell the other disciples the amazing news that Jesus was alive again.

They found the other disciples, men and women, in a room with the doors shut and presumably locked, 'for fear of the Jews'. The other disciples told them that earlier in the day Jesus had appeared to Peter. And Peter being a man, they had all believed him. The two disciples then reported that they had met Jesus on the road to Emmaus.

Jesus then materialized among them all, startling and frightening them. To prove that he was not the ghost that they thought he must be, he displayed the wounds in his hands and side and told them to feel his flesh and bones. He then ate some broiled fish that they gave him as further proof that he was real. He again explained how his death and resurrection had been foretold in the law of Moses, the prophets and the psalms, i.e. in all three parts of the Old Testament.[50] (Luke 24.44)

---

[50] In the time of Jesus The Law (Torah) included the five books of the Pentateuch (Genesis, Exodus, Leviticus, Numbers, Deuteronomy). The Prophets (Nevi'im) comprised the Former Prophets (Joshua, Judges, 1 and 2 Samuel [counted as one book], 1 and 2 Kings [counted as one book]) and the Latter Prophets (Isaiah, Jeremiah, Ezekiel, and the Twelve Minor Prophets [counted as one book]). The Writings (Ketuvim) consisted of Psalms, Proverbs, Job, the Song of Songs, Ruth, Lamentations, Ecclesiastes, Esther, Daniel, Ezra-Nehemiah [counted as one book], 1 and 2 Chronicles [counted as one book]. Thus there were 24 books in total.

The Evidence of the Resurrection

The disciple Thomas was not with them, so when they told him they had met Jesus alive he was naturally sceptical. *"Unless I see in his hands the print of the nails, and place my finger in the mark of the nails, and place my hand in his side, I will not believe,"* he said. (John 20.25) A week later Jesus reappeared to the disciples, and this time Thomas was with them. Jesus told Thomas to put his finger in the nail marks and his hand in his side, and then rebuked him for his unbelief. Thomas was embarrassed and immediately acknowledged Jesus as *"My Lord and my God!"* (John 20.28)

Jesus appeared to his disciples at intervals for another 40 days, presenting himself alive *'by many proofs… and speaking of the kingdom of God'* (Acts 1.3), until he finally left them physically at his ascension into the clouds.

Paul, writing from Ephesus to the church in Corinth 25 years later, said that after his death Jesus appeared to Peter, then to the twelve, then to more than 500 followers at one time, *'…most of whom are still alive…'* (1 Corinthians 15.6) Evidently when Paul wrote that letter there were still numerous witnesses to Jesus's resurrection who could testify to the truth of it.

The verdict of history

What do these sources tell us? In the first place the Gospel accounts have a striking ring of truth about them. While they all agree that Jesus was first dead and then fully alive, there are some apparent contradictions in the full versions, suggesting that the four writers were not regurgitating a mutually concocted story but were writing either from their own experience and recollection as eyewitnesses or from that of other independent witnesses. Their accounts include as initial evidence the testimony of several women, including Mary Magdalene who had been a prostitute, at a time when even a respectable woman's testimony was suspect in a Jewish court.[51] The male disciples in particular are presented in an unfavourable light, being rebuked several times by Jesus for their unbelief and for not having taken in what he had been prophesying about his resurrection before he died. Altogether the internal evidence strongly supports the

---

[51] Rabbi Ishmael, m. Ned. 11:10. See http://www.bible-history.com/court-of-women/women.html. Viewed June 2023.

God, Science and the Bible

conclusion that the writers were not making the story up, but were simply reporting the facts as they knew them.

Secondly it is incontrovertible, from the historical evidence I reported earlier, that Jesus's early followers believed he had risen from the dead. Preaching in Jerusalem on the morning of the day of Pentecost, Peter, who at the time of his arrest had denied even knowing Jesus, fearlessly proclaimed, *"Men of Israel, hear these words: Jesus of Nazareth, a man attested to you by God with mighty works and wonders and signs… you crucified and killed by the hands of lawless men. But God raised him up… and of that we all are witnesses."* (Acts 2.22-24,32) Later, encouraging the Christians at Corinth, Paul wrote, '*…he who raised the Lord Jesus will raise us also with Jesus and bring us with you into his presence.*' (2 Corinthians 4.14) *'If Christ has not been raised, your faith is futile…'* (1 Corinthians 15.17) It was the apostles' unshakeable belief in Christ's resurrection that motivated their preaching and took away their fear of arrest and death.

Thirdly, these early followers of Jesus must have got this belief from somewhere. Their own account of where they got this belief from is the only credible explanation. For these are the facts: Jesus *was dead.* All the historical evidence tells us that he was crucified under the jurisdiction of Pontius Pilate. No one survived a Roman crucifixion, and the soldiers on duty would have made certain he was dead before releasing his body for burial.

- <u>His body disappeared.</u> The disciples didn't have it, for if they did they would have known he was still dead and would not have believed he had risen again. The Jewish rulers didn't have it, for they were desperate to stamp out any belief in Jesus as the Messiah, and would simply have produced his body to prove that he was dead. The Romans would have done the same if they had the body, in order to suppress any possible rebellion. No one ever claimed to possess a relic of it as they have of many Christian saints. The tomb was empty and the body had disappeared.[52]

---

[52] It is claimed that the Shroud of Turin was used to wrap his body in, but even if it was, it was not a part of Jesus's body.

- <u>Jesus's disciples believed</u>. Against their own expectations, Jesus's disciples came to believe he was alive again. They were not expecting to see Jesus alive again, they were not credulous men, and they were not hallucinating. Hallucinations don't eat fish, neither can they give 40 more days of Bible teaching, that among other things equipped Peter to preach one of the most powerful sermons in history. Jesus's appearances to his followers were so convincing that they were willing to lay down their lives for testifying to the truth that he was alive again.

- <u>People who had not been his disciples believed</u>. The evidence on which they based their belief was so convincing that within a few weeks thousands of people in Jerusalem believed it too, including some of the Jewish priests, and Jesus's own natural brothers. (Acts 1.14; 2.41; 4.4; 6.7)

Several respected lawyers and people more qualified than I am in the examination of historical evidence have come to the conclusion that the only solution which fits all the facts is that Jesus did rise from the dead.[53]

Frank Morison (his real name was Albert Henry Ross) set out to write a book disproving the resurrection and he ended up convinced that it was true. First published in 1930, *Who Moved the Stone?* is such a perceptive and convincing account of historical detection that it has been reprinted continuously ever since. The latest illustrated edition (at the time of writing) was published in September 2016.

Sir Edward Clarke KC famously wrote,

> *As a lawyer, I have made a prolonged study of the evidence for the events of the first Easter Day. To me the evidence is conclusive, and over and over again in the High Court I have secured the verdict on evidence not*

---

[53] One of the most comprehensive modern summaries for the evidence of Christ's resurrection is on the website http://remnantreport.com/cgi-bin/imcart/read.cgi?article_id=238&sub=31. Viewed June 2023.

nearly so compelling. As a lawyer, I accept it unreservedly as the testimony of truthful men to facts that they were able to substantiate.[54]

Lord Darling, who conducted many famous trials and deputized for the Lord Chief Justice of England in 1918 and 1919, said at a private dinner party one evening,

> *"The crux of the problem of whether Jesus was, or was not, what he proclaimed himself to be, must surely depend upon the truth or otherwise of the resurrection. On that greatest point we are not merely asked to have faith. In its favour as a living truth there exists such overwhelming evidence, positive and negative, factual and circumstantial, that no intelligent jury in the world could fail to bring in a verdict that the resurrection story is true."*[55]

And more recently, the best-selling author Lee Strobel has concluded that *'the resurrection of Jesus Christ is the best attested event of the ancient world.*[56] That's a compelling claim from a man who was educated at Yale Law School, worked as a legal editor for the Chicago Tribune, and was an atheist until 1981.

Christ's resurrection as proof of God's existence

But what has Jesus's resurrection to do with a belief in God's existence? In the first place, as Lord Darling said, it is the proof that Jesus was who he proclaimed himself to be. If he were simply a man, a prophet or even the greatest teacher who has ever lived, his death would have been the end of him. After he had declared, *"The Son of man is to be delivered into the hands of men, and they will kill him, and he will be raised on the third day"* (Matthew 17.22,23), a failure to return to life

---

[54] In a letter to the Rev. E.L.Macassey.
[55] Quoted by Michael Green in *Man Alive!* Inter-Varsity Fellowship, September 1967. Charles John (Lord) Darling, born 6th December 1849, was a Queen's Bench judge from 1897 to 1923. He deputised for the Lord Chief Justice from 1914 to 1918. Lord Darling made this pronouncement at a private dinner party when a book about the resurrection was being discussed.
[56] *The Case for Christ: A Journalist's Personal Investigation of the Evidence for Jesus.* L.Strobel, Zondervan. Updated and expanded edition, September 2016.

The Evidence of the Resurrection

would have proved that he was a severely deluded man. But he did return to life, and his resurrection from the dead proved that he was not deluded, and that he was not simply a man.

When he said, *"For this is the will of my Father, that every one who sees the Son and believes in him should have eternal life; and I will raise him up at the last day"* (John 6.40), he clearly proclaimed himself to be the Son of God, and to have the power to restore to life anyone who believes in him. The resurrection of Jesus proves that when he said he was the Son of God he was telling the truth. *Which means of course that God was Jesus's Father, and if God was his Father then God himself must exist.*

Actually, it is obvious that no one but God could have brought someone who was so dead back to such fullness of life so miraculously. Christ's resurrection from the dead is therefore incontrovertible historical proof to anyone with an open mind that there is a God. Richard Dawkins must have known this when he wrote *The God Delusion*.[57] In the sceptical chapter entitled 'Arguments for God's Existence' Dawkins carefully avoided any mention of Christ's resurrection. His only mention of it in the book was a passing comment that resurrection was a concept 'borrowed' from other existing religions, an argument that would be considered irrelevant in any court of law and doesn't begin to satisfy the historical facts.[58]

If you want to read more about the historical evidence for Jesus Christ's existence and resurrection I recommend Josh and Sean McDowell's book, *More Than A Carpenter*, published in 2011 by Authentic Publishing. It's especially good for young people. A much more comprehensive book covering the truth of the Bible as a whole in the light of modern thought is the McDowells' book, *Evidence that Demands a Verdict—Life-Changing Truth for a Skeptical World*, published

---

[57] *The God Delusion*. R.Dawkins, Black Swan, May 2007.
[58] In the chapter headed 'Arguments for God's existence' Dawkins omitted the existence of the universe and the *origin* of species, neither of which can be explained by natural means, and he omitted the historical evidence for the resurrection of Christ. He did include a section headed 'Personal experience', but all he considered under this heading were visions, which he dismissed as hallucinations. Therefore all the arguments for God's existence that I have presented in this book Dawkins totally ignored. Presumably, he had no answer for them.

God, Science and the Bible

in 2017 by Thomas Nelson. It's intended to be a resource book for families.

As the Son of God, Jesus came to live among us for a short while to teach us the truth about his Father. Jesus is therefore the one person who can tell us with complete authority what God is like, what his purposes are for us, and what is his plan for the end of this age when his Son Jesus will return as the promised Messiah to establish at long last the everlasting kingdom of God. Like a lighthouse shining across the tumultuous waters of the centuries, the resurrection confirms that Jesus Christ was more than just an influential figure of history. It declares him unequivocally to be the Light of the World, the promised Messiah who is alive for evermore, the Son of Man, the Son of God, and '…he who is to come'. (Romans 1.1-4; Matthew 11.3) For of course, if Jesus once lived on earth as the Son of God, he can do so again.

4. The Evidence of Experience

Entering the race

I spent much of my first term as an engineering student looking for intellectual proof of God's existence, without finding any rational argument that satisfied me. But scientific truth is not based on rational arguments: it is based on facts verified by experiments. The essence of the scientific method is to devise a theory to explain something and then to conduct an experiment that will confirm or disprove it. When God, through his prophet Malachi, was rebuking his people for bringing less than a tenth of their produce to support the temple priests in their work, he said, *"Bring the full tithes into the storehouse... and thereby put me to the test, says the Lord of hosts, if I will not open the windows of heaven for you and pour down for you an overflowing blessing."* (Malachi 3.10) God was inviting his people to put him to the test, in other words, to conduct an experiment. So eventually I decided to do just that.

It was one of the hardest decisions I have ever made, because I didn't know where it would lead me. All I knew was that if there was a God who had made me, then the best possible use I could make of my life would be to discover what he had made me for and then do it. So one day, in great trepidation, I knelt down and prayed, "O God, I still don't know for certain whether you exist, but from this moment I am going to live in the belief that you do exist, and I will do whatever you tell me."

That was the day that God began to prove to me that he was real. I was filled with an extraordinary sense of peace. I found I had a new love for other people as well as for myself. In the fortnight that followed God answered every request I made to him in prayer, in two cases immediately. Jesus once said, *"...if any man's will is to do his will, he shall know whether the teaching is from God..."* (John 7.17) I have not perfectly kept the promise I made to God that day, but since then, and particularly when I have followed some clear instruction from him, God has demonstrated to me repeatedly the reality of his existence and his care for me and my family.

Thus the third way in which Christians argue the case for God's existence is from their own personal experience of him. In this chapter I'd like to share with you some of my own experiences of God. I hope this will help to explain to you why I am so sure that the God of the Bible exists. I told you earlier that my family and I once lived in Chile. It was only for 18 months, but I want to tell you why and how we got there.

"On your marks!"

In 1967 I was once again a student, this time a theological student at the beginning of my final year of training to be a Methodist minister. I was asked if I wanted to work in Britain or overseas when I left college. The pros and cons of working overseas seemed equally balanced to me, but I wanted to know what God wanted. Having never received a vision or other obvious supernatural guidance, all I could think of was to ask him to communicate with me through the Bible. After prayer, I opened my Bible at random, so far as I could. I immediately found myself reading this verse from the prophet Jeremiah: *"Am I a God at hand, says the Lord, and not a God afar off?"* (Jeremiah 23.23) I interpreted this to mean that God didn't want me to confine my service to places near at hand: he wanted people in distant lands to know him too.

Finding such a verse apparently at random may not appear to you as particularly strong evidence of God's existence, or even of his guidance. You probably think that no rational person would base the whole future course of his life on it. But you try opening the Bible at random for an answer to the question, "Should I serve God at home or abroad?" If you do it a hundred times you'll be lucky to find a single verse that could have been such a pertinent answer. (I've tried it myself as an experiment, and nothing remotely relevant came up!)

"I will do whatever you tell me." That's what I'd prayed that first day in Bristol. So my wife and I decided that I should ask for an initial 3-year post in England, in order to learn the trade as it were, and then seek an appointment abroad.

The Evidence of Experience

"Get set!"

In August 1970, a year before my first appointment as a minister in Norfolk was due to end, I arranged to visit the Methodist Missionary Society. It was to discuss my request for a stationing overseas the following year. However, before my visit to London, my wife Ann and I asked an older minister, David, to pray with us about the matter. Our idea was that we should give God the opportunity to tell us where he wanted us to go if he had somewhere particular in mind, but if he didn't make it clear then we would go wherever the folk at Mission House thought best.

We were staying in a caravan on a farm in a place called Oby, where David and I were leading a week's camp for young people. As soon as the three of us started to pray together, Ann began to see vivid pictures in her mind, as though she was looking down on a country from an aeroplane. There was an inlet from the sea, some high snow-capped mountains, a lake, a bridge, a town, a rural scene with haystacks and people at work. David apparently saw some of the same pictures in his head, for at one point he and Ann were describing the same scene together. When he then said he thought it might be Russia, my heart sank, for at that time Christians in the Soviet Union were being imprisoned. (Probably they still are.) I asked what the people looked like, and Ann was shown a sort of close-up of them. She said they were not from Africa (where I had thought we might go) nor India (which she had once thought about going to) but were more like American Indians.

Then she said, "It's South America."

"How do you know?" I asked.

"I can see a map of it," she said.

The word 'Chile' came into my mind, but I didn't say anything in case I had imagined it. Evidently the map zoomed in. It must have been like Google Maps, 45 years ahead of time.

"It's Chile!" she exclaimed.

"How do you know?" I asked again.

"It's a map of Chile. I know what a map of Chile looks like."

She described an old steam train, some native people paddling a canoe with a triangular sail, and then, more worryingly, soldiers and armoured cars.

David said, "I believe God is telling us to read Isaiah chapter 49."

"You read it and we'll listen," I replied.

David had a special gift from God. When counselling people God would sometimes drop into his mind a Bible reference such as "Isaiah 55.2", to pick a random example. Without knowing what the verse contained, David would find it, read it out and ask, "Does this mean anything to you?" And most often it did, and it would be a key to solving someone's problem. So when God told him to read Isaiah 49 he didn't immediately recall what the chapter was about. He told us afterwards that when we first asked him to pray with us about working overseas he didn't believe we should go abroad at all. So what he now read out to us must have taken him aback.

You need to know that before I was on my way into the world, my mother had two miscarriages. So when I was on the way, she prayed that if I lived I might serve God in some special way. (The prophet Samuel's mother made a similar kind of prayer before he was born—see 1 Samuel 1.11) You also need to know that Chile is 7400 miles from England, it has a Pacific coastline 2600 miles long, and it is only 217 miles wide at its widest point, making it the world's longest runner bean! It stretches down to the most southerly tip of South America at Cape Horn. Here is some of the chapter that David read out: can you see how relevant it was?

> *Listen to me, O coastlands, and hearken, you peoples from afar... The Lord says, who formed me from the womb to be his servant... "It is too light a thing that you should be my servant to raise up the tribes of Jacob and to restore the preserved of Israel; I will give you as a light to the nations, that my salvation may reach to the end of the earth."*
>
> Isaiah 49.1,5,6

As if that were not enough, we could hardly believe it when David reached verse 19: *"Surely now you will be too narrow for your inhabitants..."*!

As soon as I got home, I went to the public library and took out a book about the country. In the very first paragraph, I read, *'The name Chile is believed to come from a Mapuche word meaning "the place where the land ends," or "the end of the earth"'*! The photographs in it were just like the scenes that Ann had been shown in our time of prayer together.

A few weeks later, on 5th September 1970, Chile came into the news with the announcement that its people had elected a new president, Salvador Allende Gossens. The pictures of soldiers shown on television were like the ones Ann had seen three weeks earlier. Chile was not Russia, but it had just become the first country in the world to democratically elect a Marxist president.

Our visit to the Missionary Society in London that September was a severe disappointment. We were told that we could not go to Chile without a formal invitation from the church there, and that the British Methodist Church had no contact with the Methodist Church in Chile.

"Go!"

Seven years went by, during which I tried to contact the Chilean Methodist Church and 36 other missionary societies and organizations, all without success. Eventually in December 1977 I received a written invitation from a Chilean Pentecostal pastor to join him and his church in the city of Puerto Montt. He explained that the Chilean government would accept full-time foreign missionaries only if they were fully supported financially by their sending church or missionary society. So I took the letter to Pauline Webb, who was responsible for the Methodist Church's work in the West Indies and (so far as it existed) in South America. She told me she had just returned from Chile, where the bishop of the Methodist Church (to whom I'd written two or three years earlier without a response) had expressed a desire for closer links with British Methodism. She preferred to pursue that opening and promised to write to him about me. In August 1978, at our further request, the church's overseas service secretary, Rachel Stevens, arranged for Ann and me to attend formal interviews for overseas service in October, but she was 'not hopeful' of our being sent to Chile.

In September, I spent a day in fasting and in prayer for guidance. I wanted to know what God wanted me to do once we got to Chile. I spoke out words that I trusted God's Holy Spirit would give me, just as the prophets did. The words that came out were rather unexpected:

> *"As a master craftsman makes a key, and when it is finished he places it in a lock, and the door opens without effort, so I have made and prepared you. And when I am ready, you will open doors that have been closed for many years, and many will enter thereby and be saved."*

On the first of our two days of interviews in October, Pauline received a phone call from Juan Vasquez, the Methodist bishop of Chile. He told her he would be coming to London the following Monday for meetings of the World Methodist Council Executive. After consulting with Rachel, Pauline suggested that I should return to London to meet him at the end of that week if he expressed an interest in meeting me. Monday came and went, and the days passed by without any sign of him. He eventually turned up at Mission House unannounced, late on the Thursday evening, when the place was more or less shut up for the night. The Chilean government had been unwilling to grant him a visa to stay in England for more than 24 hours, and he had to catch a plane to Spain the next morning at 09:30. Pauline was miles away but her secretary was working late and heard the bishop's quiet knock on the adjacent office door. She sat him down in Pauline's office and wondered how to contact her boss, for in those days there were no mobile phones.

Meanwhile, Pauline was driving home along the Marylebone Road in London. Feeling tired, she said to herself, "If I see a parking meter vacant as I go by Mission House, I'll see if I can get in and make myself a cup of tea." There was one free meter right outside the locked front door. A caretaker 'happened' to be putting out some empty milk bottles at a side door and he let her in. On entering her office she was astonished to find the bishop of the Chilean Methodist Church sitting in her chair. He reiterated his desire for closer contact with the British Church. Pauline pointed to my latest letter, which was still on her desk. "This is from a Methodist minister who believes God has called him and his wife to Chile. You can have him if you want to," she said, or words to that effect.

So around 7:00 p.m. that evening, we received a frantic phone call at our home in North Yorkshire, asking me to travel overnight to meet the bishop for breakfast at his hotel. I arrived in Euston station at 2:12 a.m. and spent the rest of the night at Pauline's flat. Early next morning we drove to the hotel. There was one parking meter free outside the main entrance with 1¼ hours' prepaid parking on it. I wasn't surprised, for it was obvious that God was orchestrating everything. After detailed conversations with the bishop over breakfast, it was agreed that Ann and I, together with our four children, should be posted to Chile the following autumn.

The Evidence of Experience

We were eventually stationed in the most southerly city on mainland South America, Punta Arenas. At a nationwide conference hosted by the church there for Methodist women, a banner proclaimed in Spanish, 'Welcome to the End of the Earth.'

The finishing line

In the end, our ministry in Chile was cut short by a serious house fire and a decision by the British Methodist Church to terminate our appointment in Chile. Nevertheless, in the short time I was there, I was able to arrange several events, including Punta Arenas's first and probably only interdenominational evangelistic crusade.

As I related in the Introduction, the crusade speakers were two evangelists I invited from England, Don Double and Mike Darwood. All the local heads of General Pinochet's army, navy, air force and military police attended Saturday evening's meeting in the Municipal Theatre, along with their wives, the head of the university and the city's Roman Catholic mayor, who had made the theatre available to us. One reason for their attendance might have been the novelty of meeting English evangelists, but I think another reason was to celebrate publicly the news that the Pope had declared in favour of Chile in a dispute with Argentina about three tiny Chilean islands near Cape Horn that the Argentines claimed were theirs. So the meeting in the theatre began with heartfelt prayers of thanks to God for being on Chile's side!

Towards the end of the evening, the dignitaries and everyone else there heard testimonies from people who had given their lives to Christ on the preceding two evenings, and from some who had been physically healed through faith in Jesus. 74-year old Emiliano Kusanovic, a Croatian immigrant, came onto the stage with an amazing story. For eight months he had been unable to walk without severe pain, having fallen from a second floor window[59] while cleaning it. On the Friday evening he was helped into the Methodist Church where the crusade meeting was being held. Sitting right in front of me, he was asked if he believed that Jesus could and would heal him that night. "Yes," he replied. Mike Darwood then prayed firmly for the healing of Emiliano's leg.

---

[59] 'First floor' in British parlance.

God, Science and the Bible

The following night on stage in the theatre, Emiliano told us what happened. He was not immediately healed, but when he carefully tried to get out of bed next morning he discovered he had no pain and could walk perfectly normally. He announced to the audience in a loud voice, "I now challenge anyone in this theatre to walk better than I can!" and proceeded to stride unaided across the stage from one side to the other and back again. The audience erupted in cheers. In 2007 a square in Punta Arenas was named after him to honour a highly respected citizen.[60]

The mayor told us afterwards that he had never before felt the presence of God to be so real. Truly the Lord opened doors that would otherwise have remained closed, just as he had told me.

I could tell you about other people who were healed as a direct result of prayer while we were in Chile, and how God amazingly provided protection, guidance, money and other things, but I think I have told you enough to give some idea of why I believe so firmly that God exists. After our return to England, I began a ministry to support Chilean pastors and churches financially, as well as offering aid to victims of floods, earthquakes and volcanoes. The Chile for Christ Trust was registered as a charity in 1992 and its work continued until 2025.

---

[60] Emiliano Kusanovic was a community leader so highly respected that after his death a square in Punta Arenas was named in his honour. At the time of writing his life story can be read on the web page laprensaaustral.cl/cronica/el-cacique-de-la-18, together with a photo of him.

5. Six Thousand Years and Six Days

Science versus the Bible

Ever since Galileo, 'the father of science', was declared a heretic in 1615 for teaching that the earth went round the sun[61], there has been a kind of war between scientists and theologians, with scientists apparently on the winning side. While the Bible doesn't specifically say that the sun revolves around the earth, it seems as though the writers in general viewed the earth as resting on foundations, possibly pillars (Isaiah 48.13; Psalm 75.3), with heaven as an overarching canopy or tent. (Psalm 19.5,6; 104.2; Isaiah 40.22) But of course they might have simply been speaking poetically. After all, we sometimes speak of 'the four corners of the earth', and in Britain we speak of Australia as 'down under' when astronomically it is no more down under than we are in the northern hemisphere.

However, in the Old Testament, Job declared that God '*hangs the earth upon nothing*' (Job 26.7), and since the book of Job is generally believed to be the oldest book in the Bible, this may reflect some ancient knowledge revealed by God but later forgotten or dismissed as something impossible to believe. After all, Job could hardly have learned from personal observation that the earth was suspended in space. Job also refers to the water cycle. (Job 36.27) There is certainly nothing in the Bible as ridiculous as the belief in other ancient scriptures and folklore that the world is supported on a giant turtle or tortoise.

However most, but not all, scientists disagree strongly with what the Bible teaches on the following subjects:

---

[61] The Roman Inquisition concluded in 1615 that heliocentrism was *'foolish and absurd in philosophy, and formally heretical since it explicitly contradicts in many places the sense of Holy Scripture.'*

1. The origin of the universe
2. The origin of life
3. The age of the earth
4. The worldwide flood
5. The ages of fossils, rocks and trees

We considered the first two items in Chapter 2, and I hope I was able to convince you that neither the universe nor life as we know it could have originated out of nothing by random chance. That is the only way in which people who won't accept that God made the world supernaturally can explain its existence, and their explanations don't work.

But scientists do seem to have proof that the earth, fossils, rocks and trees are far older than the Bible implies, and they do not in general believe in the possibility of a worldwide flood as the Bible describes.

So in this chapter we'll look at the age of the earth and how long it took to make, and in the following chapters we'll look at items 4 and 5.

Why six thousand years?

According to the Hebrew Bible, on which most translations of the Old Testament are based, the world began only about four thousand years before Christ was born. The widely quoted date of 4004 BC for the creation of the world calculated by James Ussher, a former Archbishop of Ireland, is only one of many dates that people have worked out, but those based on the Hebrew Bible are all fairly similar. The Wikipedia article 'Dating creation' lists 25 calculations made by people as famous as Isaac Newton, Martin Luther and the Danish astronomer Johannes Kepler. They range from 4194 BC to 3616 BC, with an average date of 3946 BC.

Here is one relatively simple way I worked out that the calculation can be done. The book of Genesis tells us how old Adam was when his son, Seth, was born, and then carefully records the age of the father when each successive significant[62] son was born, down to the

---

[62] It is usually assumed that the genealogy is of the eldest sons, but Seth was not Adam's first son, and it seems more likely to me that these were the men

year that the Israelites settled in Egypt. (Genesis 47.7-9) Over 22 generations this gives a total of 2238 years from the creation of Adam to the settlement in Egypt. To this must be added another 11 years, because when the Bible says, for example, that Adam was 130 years old when Seth was born, he could have been any age from exactly 130 years to 130 years plus 364 days, in other words half a year older on average than the Bible says. This gives us 22 generations × 0.5 = 11 extra years, making 2249 years in total. Exodus chapter 12 verse 40 then says that the Hebrews were in Egypt for 430 years until the time of the Exodus, taking us to 2679 years from creation to the Exodus.

The most likely pharaoh at the time of the Exodus is Ramesses II. It is known that Ramesses engaged in vast building projects, for which he would have needed many slaves. His building work included the cities of Pi-Atum and his new capital Pi-Ramesses in the eastern Nile Delta. These correspond to the cities of Pithom and Raamses, which Exodus 1.11 tells us the Hebrews built. In fact Numbers 33 verses 3 and 5 tell us that they lived at Rameses, which has to have been the same place in spite of the change of spelling.

Finally, Egyptologists believe that Pharaoh Ramesses's eldest son, Amenhirwenemef, died 25 years after his father began his long reign, and if you know the Bible story you will recall that the eldest son of every Egyptian family, including Pharaoh's, died on the night of the Exodus. (Exodus 12.29; Numbers 33.4) It was the death of his son that finally persuaded the pharaoh of the Bible to allow Moses and all his people to leave Egypt.

Egyptologists differ in their estimates of the year when Ramesses II began his reign, but the consensus of most scholars is 1279 BC.[63] Adding 25 years to this gives a possible date of 1254 BC for the Exodus on the night that Pharaoh's firstborn son died. Hence 1254 + 2679 takes us back to 3933 BC for the date when the world was created, provided that:

- the Biblical records are complete and correct
- the pharaoh of the Exodus was Ramesses II

---

who figured in the genealogy of Abraham, the father of the nation of Israel, and of Moses, their first lawgiver.

[63] *The Complete Royal Families of Ancient Egypt.* As above, p. 291.

- the Egyptologists have got the date of the death of Ramesses's son right.

A date of 3933 BC is very close to the 3928 BC derived by the famous sixteenth century cartographer Gerardus Mercator. Ussher himself traced the Biblical dates beyond the Exodus to 584 BC, when the final deportation of the Jews to Babylon was known to have taken place under King Nebuchadnezzar, but he appears to have made several errors.[64]

It must be admitted that there is a historical problem with all such chronologies. According to the Bible, the First Egyptian Dynasty must have been founded after the flood, for during the flood everyone except Noah and his family drowned. However, the most commonly accepted date of 3150 BC for the start of the First Egyptian Dynasty was 873 years *before* the date of the flood based on the above calculations. I'll delve more deeply into this question in Chapter 6.

In any case it is clear that, according to the Bible, the entire universe is only about six thousand years old. In contrast, most scientists believe that the universe began 13.7 billion years ago. A number of scientific measurements and mathematical calculations can demonstrate this, and they generally agree with each other. There is probably nothing wrong with them except for one thing: they all depend on the assumption that the universe was *not* created supernaturally.

Natural or supernatural?

I'll explain what I mean by asking you a question. How do you know that everything was not created yesterday? You might reply that it could not have been created yesterday, because you can remember

---

[64] http://www.answersingenesis.org/articles/am/v1/n1/world-born-4004-bc. Viewed June 2023. See also the Wikipedia entry 'Ussher chronology'. In spite of Ussher's amazing knowledge of the Bible, Biblical languages, ancient history, ancient calendars, astronomy and chronology, he did make three known errors. He was probably trying to reach a date for creation 4000 years before the birth of Christ, which he took to have been in 5 BC.

things that you did the day before that. You might show me photos of yourself when you were born. Or a photo of your grandfather in a soldier's uniform proposing to your grandmother on Brighton pier at the end of the Second World War. But I asked, how do you know that *everything* was not created yesterday? Everything includes historical evidence and even the memories in your mind. If *everything* were created yesterday then all the evidence would still appear to prove that the world was far, far older, yet all the evidence would be wrong. If everything were no more than a day old we simply wouldn't know it.

Naturally, I am not suggesting that everything really is only a day old, although this might make the basis for a science fiction story. But suppose that the Bible's account of creation is true, I mean literally true. Suppose that God did make the heavens and the earth, trees, plants, animals, fish, birds, insects and the first man and woman in six days as the Bible tells us. And suppose you could go back in a time machine to the seventh day when everything had just been made and was all sparklingly new. All sparklingly new and *real*.

If you could prise Adam and Eve apart for a minute and examine Adam you would probably assume he was about 30 years old. If you were a dentist you might be able to prove from his teeth that he must be 30. But you would be wrong.

If you were a wood scientist you could examine one of the real trees in the Garden of Eden, take a core sample from the trunk, count the number of annual growth rings and conclude that it was perhaps 100 years old. There would be nothing wrong with your conclusion, on the assumption that the tree had grown naturally from seed. But because that assumption would be wrong your conclusion would be wrong.

If you were an astronomer and there had been enough room inside the time machine for the necessary instruments, you might be able to determine the distance of some of the stars. You might find one 10,000 light years away and conclude that it must be at least 10,000 years old for there to have been time for its light to reach the Earth. But if it had been made supernaturally only three days previously then even you would be wrong. You would be wrong because you had *assumed* that it had been made naturally rather than supernaturally.

Therefore all scientific measurements and deductions that lead to a very old age for the universe should commence with the statement, "Assuming that the universe was not created supernaturally..."

However in the Bible God consistently tells us that he did make the universe supernaturally. He made it from nothing *by his word*.

> *God said, "Let there be light"; and there was light.*
>
> Genesis 1.3

> *By the word of the Lord the heavens were made, and all their host by the breath of his mouth. ...Let all the earth fear the Lord, let all the inhabitants of the world stand in awe of him! For he spoke, and it came to be; he commanded, and it stood forth.*
>
> Psalm 33.6,8,9

> *...the world was created by the word of God, so that what is seen was made out of things which do not appear* (literally 'are not seen').
>
> Hebrews 11.3

Understanding the supernatural

Some people, even those who believe in a recent creation, will tell you that God would not have created the first tree with a hundred growth rings in it because growth rings would have been formed only if it had grown naturally. But this is to misunderstand what God did. He did not supernaturally create a *supernatural* tree. He supernaturally created a *natural* tree, a tree with roots that went right down into the ground and could only have taken years to develop naturally, a tree with a trunk so wide it must have taken 100 years to grow naturally, a tree with rings that could only have appeared after 100 years of growth, a fully natural tree of which every part was only four days old. It had to be identical in every way with the same kind of tree that grows today, if only to contain the genetic information necessary to produce another normal tree. I don't know much about genetics, but my guess is that it would have been difficult for a tree without growth rings to have produced naturally a different kind of tree that had them. The same argument goes for light from the stars. If God made a mature star 10,000 light years away from the Earth and its light did not reach the Earth it would not be a natural star. But it was a natural star and a natural universe that God made, complete in every way, functioning 100% naturally in every respect.

Since, in consequence, so many measurements of the cosmos appear to demonstrate that the universe is much older than the Bible tells us it is, one might ask, "Did God therefore deliberately deceive us?" The answer is, "No, he didn't try to deceive us. What he has made appears to be so old because there was no other way to make it. A real fully grown man or woman will inevitably appear to be 30 years old or more; a real fully grown oak tree will inevitably appear to be 100 years old or more; and a real fully formed universe has to appear to be billions of years old or it would not be a natural universe. It is a natural universe that God has created. God didn't deliberately try to trick us. There was no other way he could have done it."

Not a young Earth after all—it's six thousand years old!

In the Chapter 2, I explained why the universe and life as we know it could only have been created supernaturally. We now see that whenever this occurred, the universe would inevitably appear to be far older than it really is. The only way we could ever know how old the universe really is would be if the God who created it were to tell us. And he has told us. He has told us in the Bible.

I didn't always believe that the world began so recently. It was when I read David C.C. Watson's excellent little book, *The Great Brain Robbery*[65], that my world-view swung round 180 degrees and I realised that the Bible had to be true. The book deals principally with the theory of evolution, and among the arguments against this theory, one that particularly persuaded me was the massive evidence that human languages have *deteriorated* over the centuries, the very opposite to what would have occurred if the theory of evolution were true. Without exception, the older a language is the more complex and precise is its grammar. The Wintu Indians of California, for example, had five different forms of their verbs to distinguish whether a statement was hearsay, a result of direct observation, or had been somehow inferred, with three possible degrees of

---

[65] *The Great Brain Robbery*. D.C.C.Watson, Henry E Walter Ltd, 1975.

plausibility! Imagine listening to a court case conducted in Wintu![66] As Watson wrote, *'Everyone knows that Latin is much harder then English—cases, genders, moods, voices, personal terminations and precise syntax.* [Ancient] *Greek, perhaps 600 years older than Latin, is still more difficult; and when we come to Vedic Sanskrit in about 1500 BC the complexity is almost unbelievable.'* While all this is totally incompatible with the theory of evolution, it is just as we'd expect if God installed the original and perfect versions of human languages in people's brains at the Tower of Babel, as the Bible tells us he did, and they have gradually been deteriorating ever since.

Far from developing from grunts to grammar as evolutionary theory requires, the *facts* demonstrate that human language is deteriorating from grammar to grunts. When the English Authorized Version of the Bible was translated, the verb "to do", for example, had one form for addressing a single person ("thou dost") and another form for addressing several people ("ye do"). Now we have only one form of it ("you do"), so it is no longer so obvious whether someone is addressing everyone in a group or only one person. In several European languages, including English, we have lost in my lifetime the third person singular forms of verbs, e.g. "he does" and "she does", because people are saying simply, "they do". When that practice becomes universal we shall no longer know whether someone is talking about one person or many, male or female.

Reading David Watson's book was when my own world-view changed. I believed—really believed at last—that God created the earth and life upon it just as the Bible says he did. And as soon as I believed that, two things happened to me.

Firstly, I understood for the very first time what an amazing job God did when he designed the world and brought it into existence from nothing, with all the countless species of life that inhabit it. Secondly I realized that if God really did create the earth not so very long ago as he told us he did, then he can truly do the same again in the not so distant future, just as he has promised he will.

For the two beliefs are inextricably linked. If you can't believe that God created this present earth supernaturally as he said he did, how can you believe he will supernaturally create a new and more perfect earth as he says he will? Or if you do believe he's going to create a

---

[66] *Customs and Culture*. E.A.Nida, Harper and Brothers, New York, 1954.

The six days of creation

There's one matter that worries many theologians who believe more in conventional science than the Bible. There's no escaping the fact that the first chapter of the Bible says that God made everything in six literal days, not six long undetermined periods of time. Once again the Bible's story clashes with what most scientists believe.

Verse 5 of Genesis chapter 1 defines its use of the word 'day'. It says, *'God called the light Day, and the darkness he called Night.'* 'Day' is thus defined as the period when it is light, and 'night' when it is dark. Some people suggest that each 'day' of creation stood for a long undetermined period of time. But the rest of Genesis chapter 1 defines still more carefully what it meant by the word 'day'. After each day of creation it says, *'And there was evening and there was morning, one day.'* Jews still reckon that each new day begins in the evening at sunset. The writer was evidently explaining in a way that no one could misunderstand that he was talking about six literal 24-hour days.

When God later gave his people the Ten Commandments he told them to work for six days every week and to rest every seventh day because, he said, that is what he had done when he created the world. If he had really taken billions of years to create the world then he would have been lying to them.

The same Hebrew word for 'day' used in Genesis chapter 1 occurs in its singular form another 1150 times in the Old Testament. In this form it *never* means a long period of time. To pretend that it means a long period of time only in the first chapter of the Bible is sheer make-believe.[67]

---

[67] The German Professor Gerhard von Rad was an acknowledged linguistic expert who published a famous commentary on Genesis in 1960. He regarded the six-day creation story as a primitive and mistaken idea, yet he wrote, *'Unquestionably the days are* [intended] *to be regarded as literal days of 24 hours.'*

The only reason for believing that the days in Genesis chapter 1 stood for six long periods of time is that most scientists believe the universe took far longer than six days to evolve. But as we've already seen, scientific calculations of the age of the universe are all based on the assumption that it was not created supernaturally. Therefore the only reason not to believe that the world was created in six literal days is that many people believe the world was not created in six literal days!

A strange order of events

Nevertheless, the order in which the first chapter of Genesis tells us that God brought things into existence is difficult to understand from any natural point of view. It tells us that there was first water. (Genesis 1.2,6) It then says that God made everything else in the following order:

Day 1: Light
Day 2: A 'firmament' called heaven that separated the water above and below it
Day 3: Dry land and seas, and vegetation of all kinds: plants yielding seed according to their own kinds, and trees bearing fruit in which is their seed, each according to its kind
Day 4: The sun, moon and stars
Day 5: Sea creatures and birds
Day 6: Land creatures and human beings

It is true that if God had created everything naturally, much of this would be nonsensical. Where did this water come from that he had to separate into two parts? How could there have been light before he made the sun and the other stars to provide it? How could the first day have had a morning and evening before the earth existed?

One day as I was praying, a picture came into my mind. It was a picture of a painting, and the painting showed a stream flowing over a waterfall and down into a pool. God showed me that in real life the stream must have come first, for there could be no waterfall without a stream to supply it. And in real life the waterfall must have come before the pool did, for there would have been no water to fill the pool without a waterfall. But the painting was not real life: it was only a painting of real life. So the artist could have painted each part in any order he chose. He could have painted the pool first if he had chosen to. In a sense, he was creating the stream and waterfall and pool supernaturally. So the order in which he painted each part did not have to correspond to their natural order of creation. Indeed, he could have finished the picture by painting the sun, even though the rest of the scene was already in daylight.

Since God created everything supernaturally he could do it in any way and in any order he chose. Perhaps the original water was the canvas or workbench on which he operated. An artist would not consider the canvas as part of his picture, so maybe that's why God didn't include the water in his items of creation.

Nevertheless let's examine the apparent anomalies in the account of creation a little more closely. People who have had near-death experiences of heaven—totally real experiences of being in a heavenly realm while their bodies were clinically dead—such people frequently refer to the dazzling light that seems to permeate everything they look at.

Brad Barrows, for example, had been blind from birth. At the age of eight, severe pneumonia stopped his heart beating for four minutes. In his spirit he was taken to a beautiful field with very tall grass and palm trees that he could see! *"There was tremendous light up there,"* he told two researchers some years later. *'It seemed to come from every direction... It seemed like everything, even the grass I had been stepping on, seemed to soak in that light.'*[68]

Captain Dale Black, a commercial airline pilot, was taking off in a twin-engined Piper Navajo when it suddenly lost power and crashed into a stone monument. He found himself alive, but suspended in mid-air above his shattered body. Two angels led him to a magnificent city. *"The entire city was bathed in light, an opaque whiteness in which the light was intense but diffused... It didn't shine on things but through them. Through the grass. Through the trees. Through the walls. And through the people who were gathered there..."*[69]

---

[68] *Mindsight: Near-Death and Out-of-Body Experiences in the Blind.* K.Ring & S.Cooper, Institute of Transpersonal Psychology, 1999.
[69] *Flight to Heaven.* Dale Black, Bethany House Publishers, May 2010.

God, Science and the Bible

So does it still seem so unlikely the first thing God said in his week of creation was, *"Let there be light"*? Perhaps the light was simply a manifestation of the energy that he would need to power everything else he made.

What about time? How could there have been a 24-hour day with morning and evening before a rotating earth was created? Before God began his work of physical creation he made both space and time. The phrase 'in the beginning' indicates that the first thing he did was to create time, for without time there could have been no beginning of anything. Therefore it was not the Earth's rotation that defined the length of a day, but it was the length of a day that defined how fast God had to make the Earth rotate in order to complete one rotation in a day.

It is true that the account of separating water above and below the earth with a 'firmament' or 'expanse' called heaven and then gathering the water underneath the firmament into seas in order to expose the dry land seems to describe an earth that is very different to the one we know now. But once again, a supernatural process of creation does not have to bear a direct relationship to the finished product once it is converted into the real thing. My guess is that a parallel situation would be the kind of explanation a mother might give to her four-year-old son who asks how he was made. "I grew you in my tummy" would not be the whole explanation and would not be strictly accurate, but it would be the most that a small boy could understand.

If all this still doesn't satisfy you I've provided an original and radically different explanation of God's six days of creation in Annex 1. It may be of interest to more scientifically minded readers.

Genesis 2.7 says, '...*the Lord God formed man of dust from the ground, and breathed into his nostrils the breath of life; and man became a living being.*' God created the first man supernaturally, but only when he was complete did he become a living, natural, human being. This suggests to me that the Lord first created everything supernaturally in ways beyond our natural understanding, and then, when everything was ready, when he was satisfied that the picture he had painted so to speak was complete, he brought it all to natural life by the power of his Spirit. From that moment onwards it functioned naturally.

6. The Universal Flood

The Bible's account

In the six hundredth year of Noah's life, in the second month, on the seventeenth day of the month, on that day all the fountains of the great deep burst forth, and the windows of the heavens were opened. And rain fell upon the earth forty days and forty nights... And the waters prevailed so mightily upon the earth that all the high mountains under the whole heaven were covered; the waters prevailed above the mountains, covering them fifteen cubits deep. And all flesh died... everything on the dry land in whose nostrils was the breath of life died... Only Noah was left, and those that were with him in the ark. From Genesis 7.11-24

Whole books have been written on this subject, both for and against the belief that such a universal flood really occurred. I can hardly enter into such a huge debate at this point. But since Jesus clearly believed that the Flood occurred and that Noah built the ark as described (Matthew 24.37-39), I'll content myself with just a few points which I hope cannot be contradicted, in support of the account in Genesis.

The Genesis Flood

The Genesis Flood, written by John Whitcomb and Henry Morris back in 1961, was the first book to address seriously the conflict between the Bible's account of the Flood and generally accepted science. It was republished in 2012 as a fiftieth anniversary edition,[70] so it must still have some value. One of the few unbiased reviewers of the book on Amazon said it provides an excellent summary of the creationist

---

[70] *The Genesis Flood, The Biblical Record and its Scientific Implications, 50th Anniversary Edition.* J.C.Whitcomb & H.M.Morris, Presbyterian and Reformed, 2012.

standpoint on the subject of the Flood. Here are just five of the points that the authors make, in slightly simplified form:

- If all the water in our present atmosphere were suddenly precipitated, it would cover the ground to an average depth of less than 2 inches (5cm). A global rainfall continuing for 40 days would have required a completely different mechanism for its production than what is available at the present day. However Genesis 1.7 speaks of 'the waters that were above the firmament'. If prior to the Flood there was a high-altitude canopy of water vapour free from the particles that are a necessary precursor to precipitation as water droplets, the resulting increased absorption of the sun's radiation and the more uniform distribution of the resulting heat would have produced a uniformly warm temperature over the Earth prior to the Flood. This would explain the widespread existence of fossils of temperate and semi-tropical plants and animals even near the poles.[71] It could also explain why Genesis tells us that it did not rain until after the Flood. (Genesis 2.5,6; 7.12) Today the temperature in the thermosphere 80 miles above the Earth is very high, conducive to retaining large amounts of water vapour, and water vapour is lighter than air so the existence of such a water vapour canopy prior to the Flood seems perfectly possible.

If water then covered the whole earth to a depth of 'fifteen cubits (25 feet) above the mountains', where did it go when the flood subsided? Psalm 104.6-9 answers the question. It describes how God reshaped the earth's surface after the Flood, raising what had previously been relatively low mountains and sinking what had previously been relatively shallow valleys:

---

[71] *'The general distribution and character of the rocks and their fossil content point to more uniform climatic conditions that those of today. Fossils in the Arctic Silurian rocks are not essentially different from those of low latitudes.'* W.J.Miller: *An Introduction to Historical Geology*, 6th edition, Van Nostrand, 1952, p.116. Similar statements made in geological textbooks about the Miocene, Cambrian, Ordovician, Devonian and Carboniferous eras are quoted in *The Genesis Flood*, cited above.

The Universal Flood

Thou didst cover [the earth] *with the deep as with a garment; the waters stood above the mountains. At thy rebuke they fled; at the sound of thy thunder they took to flight. The mountains rose, the valleys sank down to the place which thou didst appoint for them. Thou didst set a bound which they should not pass, so that they might not again cover the earth.*

There is plenty of evidence from fossil finds and echo-sounding equipment that both these events actually happened.[72] Canyons deep below the surface of the ocean, but presumably originally carved out by rivers above the ground, occur all over the world.[73] Near the mouth of the Hudson River they are nearly 3 miles below the surface.[74] The psalm also makes it easier to understand how all the mountains could have been covered with water during the Flood: they were not nearly so high as they are now.

- A universal flood offers a credible explanation for the formation of sedimentary rocks. Sedimentary rocks are rocks which have been deposited as sediments, which the *Oxford Universal Dictionary on Historical Principles* defined as 'earthy or detrital matter deposited by aqueous agency'. Obviously these great masses of sediments must first have been eroded from some previous location, transported, and then deposited, perhaps on more than one occasion—exactly the sort of thing which occurs in any flood and must have occurred on a uniquely grand scale during the great flood of Genesis.

---

[72] Fossils of whales and other sea creatures have been found high in the mountains of Chile and California. In 2015 oil prospectors using echo-sounding equipment discovered a 1.2-mile deep landscape in the North Atlantic west of the Orkney-Shetland Islands, with peaks that once belonged to mountains and eight major rivers. Researcher Nicky White, from University of Cambridge, said: "It looks for all the world like a map of a bit of a country onshore." *Lost world: Ancient submerged landscape of mountains and riverbeds found on the Atlantic seabed.* Daily Mail, July 2011.
[73] *Submarine Geology*. F.P.Shepard, Harpers New York, 1948.
[74] *Principles of Geomorphology*. W.D.Thornbury, Wiley, 1954.

- A universal flood offers the best explanation of how fossils were formed. In general, fossils are found only in sedimentary rocks. (You can't insert a mammoth into a block of granite.) Tens of thousands of extinct animals, many of them mammoths, have been found preserved whole, with even flesh and hair intact, particularly in Siberia. This could only have happened without their decaying or being eaten by scavengers if they were buried suddenly in the sediments they have been found in.[75] Similarly the fossilization of many kinds of fish is indicative of very rapid burial and solidification, for in normal circumstances a dead fish is eaten by other fish or sea creatures.[76]

- In particular a sudden universal flood offers the most rational explanation for the extinction of the dinosaurs. If every creature not aboard the ark was drowned, and if no dinosaur pairs were aboard the ark, then their sudden extinction was inevitable. In August 2017 the *Guardian* newspaper reported the findings of a paper published by the Royal Society about an unusual dinosaur called the Chilesaurus.[77] The *Guardian* article explained:

    Dinosaurs were the monarchs of Earth for 160 million years until a space rock collided with the planet 65.5m years ago and wiped out those confined to land. Ornithischia thrived for more than 100 million years, but were wiped out when the rogue rock smashed into what today is the Yucatan peninsula in Mexico. The impact probably created a massive firestorm followed by a

---

[75] See for *example* the Wikipedia entry, 'Fossils of the Burgess Shale'.

[76] '*Several garpike, ranging in size from 4 to 6 feet, have been disentombed, as have birds of about the size of the domestic chicken and resembling the snipe or plover in general conformation. In addition, specimens of sunfish, rasp-tongues, deep sea bass, chubs, pickerel and herring have been found, not to mention mollusca, crustaceans, birds, turtles, mammals and many varieties of insects.*' Deposits found in Lincoln County, Wyoming, described in '*Fishing for Fossils*', Compressed Air Magazine, Volume 63, March 1958, p.24.

[77] *A dinosaur missing link? Chilesaurus and the early evolution of ornithischian dinosaurs.* M.G.Baron & P.M.Barrett, Biology Letters, The Royal Society, 16 August 2017. DOI: 10.1098/rsbl.2017.0220.

decades-long winter that destroyed vegetation, the starting point in the dinosaurs' food chain.

Quite apart from the extraordinary notion that a rock falling in Mexico could wipe out dinosaurs all over the earth by destroying the starting point of their food chain and presumably all the intermediate life forms at the same time, the scientific paper that the article was supposedly reporting said nothing of the sort. The explanation of the dinosaurs' extinction was pure fiction, made to sound like fact in the context of a genuine scientific paper. Many of the 'facts' that we are told emanate not from scientists but from journalists writing for attention-seeking editors.

- A universal flood perfectly explains the most common order of fossilized life forms found in the standard geologic column. When the fountains of the deep broke up and the heavens above broke open, the first creatures to be affected would have been sea creatures. Invertebrate sea creatures (molluscs, etc.) would have been buried first in the tide of debris and mud that swept into the shallow seas, then vertebrates (fish etc.) would have been buried, after they had tried to swim to safety. Then, as the flood waters filled the lower-lying land, amphibians would have been trapped, then the slower moving reptiles, then animals (which could initially have escaped to higher ground), and finally birds, which presumably flew around until they died of hunger. This also explains why trilobites, for example, are never found in the same layer as dinosaurs.

The fountains of the deep

The one aspect of the Flood that the authors of *The Genesis Flood* don't seem to have addressed is this matter of the 'fountains of the great deep.' The phrase suggests that vast quantities of water were previously trapped under pressure beneath the surface of the earth and burst out. That is certainly what Walter Brown believes,[78] although much of what he says has been strongly refuted by people who don't believe the Biblical account.[79] However scientists working with the Hubble Space Telescope in 2016 excitedly reported observations that strongly supported the possibility of water being trapped under pressure below the surface of a planet. They identified fountains of water or ice spewing 100 miles into space from the surface of Europa, one of Jupiter's moons. A report on *USA Today* stated, '*Water from this salty sea presumably shoots up through cracks in the outer coating of ice, which measures tens of miles thick or more.*' NASA's Curtis Niebur admitted they didn't have a full explanation for the process. *"We're seeing* [the plumes] *using a completely different technique. That gives you a lot more evidence that it's not just a fluke, that it's actually something physical.*'[80]

Even on the earth today geysers of water such as 'Old Faithful' in the Yellowstone National Park continue to spout water into the air; oil spurts out of the ground when it is released; and volcanoes can eject ash 20 miles upwards into the sky. If water was once trapped beneath the earth's crust and was superheated by volcanic magma the generated pressure could well have been explosive.

A universal belief

Ancient cultures all over the world have independently handed down a story about a great flood that once took place. Wikipedia's entry 'List of flood myths' lists 38 such stories from China and the Far East, India and the Middle East, Europe, North and South America, Africa and even Polynesia and Hawaii. Why is there such a universal belief in a universal flood if such a flood never occurred? Here's one such story from the Philippines. It can hardly have been based on the Biblical story, yet it has elements that clearly match the Biblical account:

---

[78] *In the Beginning: Compelling Evidence for Creation and the Flood.* W.Brown, Center for Scientific Creation, August 2008.

[79] *Walter Brown's "Hydroplate" Flood Model Doesn't Hold Water.* G.J.Kuban, http://paleo.cc/ce/wbrown.htm. Viewed June 2023.

[80] *Scientists find incredible fountains shooting from Jupiter's moon.* T.Watson, *USA TODAY*, 26 September, 2016

The Universal Flood

Once upon a time, when the world was flat and there were no mountains, there lived two brothers, sons of Lumawig, the Great Spirit. The brothers were fond of hunting, and since no mountains had formed there was no good place to catch wild pig and deer. The older brother said: "Let us cause water to flow over all the world and cover it, and then mountains will rise up."

Here are two more stories. An ancient Celtic myth from Wales tells of a great flood caused by the monster Afanc who dwelt in Llyn Llion, which was possibly Bala Lake. All humans were drowned except Dwyfan and Dwyfach. They escaped in a huge mastless boat or ark called *Nefyd Naf Neifion*, on which they carried two of every living kind. From Dwyfan and Dwyfach all the island of Prydain (Britain) was repopulated.

In Inca mythology the creator god, Viracocha, arose out of Lake Titicaca and made mankind by breathing into stones. His first creations were brainless giants who displeased him, so he destroyed them with a flood and made better people from smaller stones.

Once again, why would people all over the world who had no contact with the Bible believe that there had once been a universal flood, if it never occurred? All these myths have some similarities to the Biblical account, yet none of them seems quite so rational. In my opinion the only 'myth' that the Wikipedia article should not have included in its list is the Biblical account of what actually happened.

Egyptian chronology and the date of the flood

The generally accepted date for the first Egyptian dynasty is earlier than the date of the Flood according to Biblical chronology.

In Chapter 5, I showed how according to Biblical chronology the world was created roughly around the year 3933 BC. I explained how the genealogies in Genesis enable us to calculate that the Exodus took place 2679 years after creation. In the same way it can be calculated that the Flood occurred 1656 years after creation, which would give us a date for the Flood of 2277 BC. (In my book, *The Date of Christ's Return*, I derive a more accurate date of 3967 BC for creation according to the Bible, which gives a Biblical date of 2311 BC for the Flood.)

God, Science and the Bible

Now the Bible tells us that the following year there were only eight people alive on the earth: Noah, his wife, their three sons and their sons' wives. Yet according to Egyptologists Dodson and Hilton[81], the First Dynasty of Egypt is conjectured to have begun in 3150 BC, 839 years *before* the Flood!

Although the names of some 300 Egyptian kings are known, dating them is notoriously difficult. Some surviving lists of kings cover many rulers but have significant gaps in their text; others provide a complete list of rulers for only a short period of Egyptian history. Some Egyptian dynasties may have overlapped, with different kings ruling in different regions at the same time rather than serially. Since the next conjectural date after the establishment of the first dynasty in 3150 is that of the final ruler of the second dynasty (the unfortunately named Nebwyhetepimyef, 2611-2584 BC), I am of the opinion that the earlier date of 3150 BC is somewhat speculative. 2611 BC however would be exactly 300 years after the Flood.

While Dodson and Hilton's book sets out the consensus of most scholars, there are a number of alternative chronologies. The 'New Chronology' was developed by the English Egyptologist David Rohl and other researchers in the 1990s. It sets the later New Kingdom dates as much as 350 years later.[82] Rohl asserts that the New Chronology allows him to identify some of the characters in the Hebrew Bible with people whose names appear in archaeological finds.

Another chronology was published privately in 1971 by Donovan Courville in his 700-page two-volume book *The Exodus Problem and Its Ramifications: A Critical Examination of the Chronological Relationships Between Israel and the Contemporary Peoples of Antiquity*.[83] He concluded that Egypt was founded around 2300 BC, which would have been shortly after the Flood date according to the Bible.

In summary, it is difficult but not impossible to reconcile the early history of Egypt with the chronology of the Bible.

---

[81] The *Complete* Royal Families of Ancient Egypt. A.Dodson & D.Hilton, Thames and Hudson, 2010.

[82] *A Test of Time*. D.Rohl, Cornerstone, 2001.

[83] See the Wikipedia article on 'Donovan Courville'.

7. The Fossil Record

Radioactive carbon dating

Radioactive carbon (C_{14}) is extensively used to determine the age of things that once lived, so in theory it should be possible to determine the age of fossils by radiocarbon dating.

This is how it works. High-energy cosmic radiation from the sun continually changes nitrogen atoms in the upper atmosphere into radioactive carbon atoms.[84] These combine with atmospheric oxygen to form radioactive carbon dioxide. Plants absorb the resulting mixture of normal carbon dioxide and radioactive carbon dioxide from the air and use it to build their cells. Living creatures then eat the plants and absorb the carbon. As a result, a tiny proportion (something like one part per trillion) of the carbon in all living things is radioactive, the same proportion as the radioactive carbon in the air. You are slightly radioactive!

When a plant or animal dies, it stops absorbing carbon from the air but the radioactive carbon already in it continues to decay at a known rate. So from its known 'half-life' of about 5730 years, the relative amount of radioactive carbon that remains in a fossil, mummy, gatepost, or dress made from natural fibres can be used to determine how old it is. For example, if the proportion of radioactive carbon in the carbon content is only half what it is in the atmosphere then the object is 5730 years old or thereabouts, always assuming that

---

[84] A cosmic ray in the form of a high-energy proton (a positively charged particle) collides with an atom in the *atmosphere* converting one of its neutrons into a separate high-energy ('thermal') neutron. This in turn collides with a nitrogen atom in the atmosphere, replacing a proton and converting it to radioactive carbon. N_{14} (7 protons + 7 neutrons) + 1 thermal neutron = C_{14} (6 protons + 8 neutrons) + 1 proton.

God, Science and the Bible

the proportion of C_{14} in the atmosphere has remained fairly constant throughout that period.[85]

However, while radiocarbon dating has been used with reasonable success on items from Egyptian tombs known to be around 4700 years old it is *not* used on fossils, for the simple reason that the relative quantities of C_{14} remaining in them are too small to be measured accurately. Of course this is put down to the fact that fossils must be extremely old. In fact the oldest fossils are believed to be about 3.5 billion years old. But does the near absence of C_{14} in fossils really prove that they are extremely old?

Peter's prediction

In my youth I visited the caves in Cheddar Gorge in Somerset. In one place a cluster of small white stalactites, illuminated by imaginative lighting, was silently reflected in a black pool of water beneath them that looked for all the world like some stunningly beautiful Tolkienian city. In another place a guide told us that a massive stalactite suspended above the passageway and still dripping water from its tip was so many thousands of years old. I asked her how she knew its age. She explained that its rate of growth had been measured over several years so it was possible to calculate when it first began to form from its current size. The question that immediately came to my mind was "How do they know that it always grew at the same rate?" I was not confident enough at that age to ask her, but it did seem to me that in earlier centuries or millennia the watercourse on the surface might have changed direction, or the mineral content of the water might have changed. A similar question could justifiably be asked about the apparent age of fossils when an

---

[85] The historical proportions of C_{14} in the atmosphere have been measured from the rings of ancient trees. Carbon in a tree trunk is absorbed only in the outer ring each year, so each tree ring gives an estimate of the proportion of C_{14} in the atmosphere in the year it grew, after an allowance has been made for radioactive decay corresponding to its age. In recent history the widespread burning of fossil fuels reduced the proportion of C_{14} in the atmosphere, and the atmospheric nuclear tests conducted in the 1950s and 1960s almost doubled it for a while. Claims that trees can provide data going back 13,900 years seem very dubious to me.

The Fossil Record

attempt is made to date them from their C_{14} content. How does one know that C_{14} has always been present in the atmosphere in similar amounts throughout their life?

If the Biblical account of the Flood is correct and if, prior to the Flood, there was a vast amount of water above the earth, presumably as water vapour, it could and probably would have shielded atmospheric nitrogen from cosmic rays. This would have prevented the production of C_{14}, either in part or entirely, so that anything living before the Flood would have absorbed little or no C_{14}. Therefore every living thing fossilized as a result of the Flood would inevitably have appeared to be far, far older than it really is.[86] The presence of 'the waters which were above the firmament' mentioned in Genesis chapter 1 destroys the validity of radiocarbon dating when it is applied to fossils created by the Flood, and to anything that grew in the years immediately after the Flood while C_{14} levels in the atmosphere began to build up. And if it was the Flood that buried all the now fossilized plants and animals, the apparent great age of fossils determined by measurements of C_{14} cannot be presented as proof that the earth is a day older than the Bible indicates it is.[87]

Nearly 2000 years ago the apostle Peter wrote, '...*scoffers will come in the last days... saying, "...all things have continued as they were from the beginning of creation." They deliberately ignore this fact, that... the world that then existed was deluged with water and perished.*' (2 Peter 3.3-6) It's almost

---

[86] Coal, which is fossilized wood, contains variable amounts of C_{14}, which are normally explained as originating from the radioactive decay of the uranium-thorium isotope series that is naturally found in rocks. Since some coal has no measurable C_{14} I wonder whether all the C_{14} detected in other fossils comes not from the absorption of C_{14} while they were alive before the Flood but from contamination by other radioactive elements in the surrounding rock.

[87] It is true that a paper published in 1986 by Linick and others in the journal *Radiocarbon* reported that radiocarbon ages were consistently found to be only 15% less than the ages of samples of dead bristlecone pine trees dated back to 6554 BC, but the methods used to date ancient bristlecone pine trees are based on a false assumption, as will be explained later. It is also claimed that radiocarbon dating can be verified 45,000 years back by checking its results against the known dates of cave formations called speleothems, but these 'known' dates were derived by uranium-thorium radioactivity measurements which are also based on a false assumption, as I shall explain ion Chapter 8.

as though Peter foresaw how scientists today would ignore the effect of the Flood on radiocarbon dating!

Determining the age of fossils from the geological column

As I explained earlier, C_{14} is not used to determine the age of fossils because too little radioactive carbon remains in them to obtain a reliable value. So how do scientists know, or think they know, how many years ago a dinosaur or trilobite lived? If you are very bright you might guess that they measure instead the age of the rock in which the fossil is embedded, using one of the other kinds of radioactivity I mentioned earlier. But they can't do that because fossils are almost always found in sedimentary rock—rock that has been laid down by sand and mud sediments washed down by water—and sedimentary rock doesn't contain any radioactive elements that might be used to date it. So how on earth is the age of a fossil known? The answer is, it isn't! Let me explain...

Most people are probably familiar with the geological column that appears in school textbooks and reference books all over the world.[88] A simplified version of this is shown in Figure 1. (The original diagram is public domain from the US National Park Service.)

---

[88] At the time of writing the web page creationwiki.org/Geological_column has a good explanation of the geological column.

The Fossil Record

Figure 1: The geological column, simplified

MILLIONS OF YEARS AGO	PERIOD		REPRESENTATIVE LIFE
		Quaternary Period	
CENOZOIC ERA ("Recent Life") 1½ – 65	Tertiary Period		Primitive horses
MESOZOIC ERA ("Middle Life") 65 – 140	Cretaceous Period		Last dinosaurs
140 – 210	Jurassic Period		Quarry Dinosaurs
210 – 245	Triassic Period		First Dinosaurs
PALEOZOIC ERA ("Ancient Life") 245 – 290	Permian Period		Priimitive Reptiles
290 – 320	Pennsylvanian Period		Giant Insects
320 – 360	Mississippian Period		Brachiopods
360 – 410	Devonian Period		Primitive Fishes
410 – 440	Silurian Period		"Sea Scorpions"
440 – 500	Ordovician Period		Nautiloids
500 – 570	Cambrian Period		Trilobites

Fossils older than Cambrian are rare.
This earlier span of time is usually called simply Precambrian.

I had always assumed, as perhaps other people do, that words like 'Cretaceous', 'Devonian' and 'Cambrian' applied to different kinds of rock, and that it was somehow known how old these rocks were, and therefore how old the fossils in them were. But it's nothing like that. The different strata of rock are simply named after the places where the corresponding kinds of fossils were first found, and the ages assigned to the *rocks* are assigned from the assumed ages of the *fossils*.

In the early 1800s, the English canal builder William Smith noticed that similar fossils were generally found in the same kind of strata throughout England, and that the different kinds of strata were generally found in the same sequence. He also noticed that smaller and less complex fossils tended to be found in lower layers, and larger and more complex organic remains in the higher layers. It was assumed that the lower layers had been laid down first and that therefore the fossils in them were older than the ones in higher layers. Secondly, on the assumption that the theory of evolution was true, it was concluded that many millions of years must have elapsed between the formation of each layer to give time for the successive stages of evolution to take place. Eventually, by assessing radiometrically the ages of adjacent layers of non-sedimentary rocks (on the assumption that they were not created supernaturally), some supposedly more accurate timescales were assigned to the various periods of time.

In order to compare rock strata in various parts of the world, a system of 'index fossils' was then set up to identify each stratum. An index fossil is a type of fossil that is easily identifiable and reasonably plentiful.[89] Furthermore, it is a fossil that occurs in only one layer of rock at any particular location. That implies that it didn't come into existence before that layer was formed, and that it went out of existence before the layer above it was formed, once again on the assumption that the theory of evolution is a fact. Having assigned a set of index fossils to each assumed period of the Earth's age, they were then used to identify similar rock strata in other geological sites around the world and to assign the corresponding ages to them.[90] Whenever a new kind of fossil is discovered now, it is immediately dated from the age that has been assigned to the rock stratum in

---

[89] Corals, graptolites, brachiopods, trilobites, and echinoids (sea urchins) are examples of index fossils.

[90] *Fossil Frustrations*. D.V.Ager, New Scientist, Vol. 100, 10 November 1983, p. 425. '*Ever since William Smith at the beginning of the 19th century, fossils have been and still are the best and most accurate method of dating and correlating the rocks in which they occur. ... Apart from very 'modern' examples, which are really archaeology, I can think of no cases of radioactive decay being used to date fossils.*'

The Fossil Record

which it is found. Thus to some extent fossils are used to date rocks and the rocks are then used to date fossils![91]

The result of all this is the geological column, which many scientists and most of the public now accept as a fact. So why did I say that the ages of fossils are not known?

Unprovable assumptions

In the first place the construction of the geological column is based on unprovable assumptions.

The idea that the lower strata in a rock formation must have been laid down millions of years before the higher strata is based on the assumptions that the theory of evolution is true and that there was never a universal flood. However no one has been able to produce any evidence of evolution taking place, and a universal flood provides an obvious explanation for the most common sequence of fossil layers, which could therefore all have been formed within a few months of each other.

As we have seen, the assumption that the approximate ages of adjacent rocks can be determined radiometrically assumes that they were formed naturally rather than supernaturally, which is again an unprovable assumption. In Chapter 2 I explained why the earth could not have evolved naturally. It could not have been formed out of ever-expanding gases in accordance with the known behaviour of gases, nor ended up rotating on its axis in a circuit around the sun in accordance with the known laws of motion.

The geological column is falling apart

In the second place, increasing knowledge about fossils is knocking holes in the geological column. Since it was first set up, more and

---

[91] *Pragmatism Versus Materialism in Stratigraphy.* J.E.O'Rourke, American Journal of Science, Vol. 276, January *1976*, p. 47. '*The intelligent layman has long suspected circular reasoning in the use of rocks to date fossils and fossils to date rocks. The geologist has never bothered to think of a good reply, feeling that explanations are not worth the trouble as long as the work brings results. This is supposed to be hard-headed pragmatism.*'

more fossils have been turning up in 'wrong' places.[92,93] Former index fossils such as Camptochlamys have been found in one stratum in one country and in a different stratum from a supposedly completely different geological period in another. In just ten years between 1982 and 1992 Sepkoski identified 1026 families of fossils that had apparently begun living earlier than was first believed or had continued living later than was originally believed, and could therefore no longer be used as index fossils to date a single period of time.[94] Some former index fossils, such as the coelacanth fish, which was believed to have died out 65 million years ago with the dinosaurs, have even turned up alive and well today![95]

> *Since* Lystrosaurus *has always been used to correlate rocks into time-equivalent horizons, and to place them into the Early Triassic, the Permian find of* Lystrosaurus *should now mean that Permian and Triassic are contemporaneous! An analogous line of reasoning should lead to the position that Cretaceous and Tertiary are now contemporaneous because the Upper Cretaceous genus* Parafusus *is now known from Early Tertiary rocks.*
>
> *Of course, the uniformitarians would never follow their own reasoning to its logical conclusion... In order to paper over this fatal flaw in the geologic column, uniformitarians simply back-pedal, discard* Lystrosaurus *as well as other once-esteemed index fossils as time-stratigraphic indicators, choose other index fossils as presumed time-indicators, and otherwise act as if nothing has happened in terms of empirical evidence. This enables them to go right on believing in such things*

---

[92] *Evolution pushed further into the past.* M.J.Oard, CEN Technical Journal, 10(2), pp.171–172, 1996.

[93] *How well do palaeontologists know fossil distribution?* M.J.Oard, CEN Technical Journal, 14(1), pp.7–8, 2000.

[94] *A compendium of fossil marine animal families.* J.J.Sepkoski, 2nd edition, Milwaukee Public Museum Contributions *to* Biology and Geology No. 83, p. 7, 1992.

[95] *The Coelacanth: More Living than Fossil.* Smithsonian National Museum of Natural History. vertebrates.si.edu/fishes/coelacanth/coelacanth_wider, viewed September 2017.

The Fossil Record

as the Permian, Triassic, Cretaceous, and Tertiary periods. Heads I win, tails you lose.[96]

There have been several discoveries in recent years—notably in 2005 and 2015—of dinosaur bones that still contained flexible tissue and blood cells.[97,98] It is generally accepted that when an animal dies, soft tissues such as blood vessels, muscle and skin decay and disappear over time, so these discoveries make it extremely unlikely that the last dinosaur disappeared from the earth a massive 65 million years ago as the geological column insists! On the other hand, the drowning and fossilization of dinosaurs in a worldwide flood a mere 4300 years ago or so seems far more plausible.

The fossil record supports creation, not evolution

It must be evident to any unbiased observer that the fossil record supports a belief in the Biblical account of creation rather than the theory of evolution. For one thing, if the rocks have existed since the earliest forms of life and if they contain a record of the evolution of life from its beginning until recent times then there should be a complete record of life forms from simple to complex, including multitudes of intermediate forms linking consecutive evolutionary stages. Such a record simply doesn't exist. Darwin himself acknowledged this when he wrote, '*Why, if species have descended from other species by insensibly fine gradations, do we not everywhere see innumerable transitional forms? Why is not all nature in confusion instead of species being, as we see them, well defined?*'[99]

The answer, of course, was that his theory was wrong, but Darwin could only surmise that the fossil record in his day must have been '*incomparably less perfect than is generally supposed*'. However, that

---

[96] *The fossil record: Becoming more random all the time.* J.Woodmorappe, Creation Ministries International. creation.com/the-fossil-record, viewed September 2017.
[97] *The real Jurassic Park.* S.Doyle, Creation 30(3) pp.12–15, 2008.
[98] *Fibres and cellular structures preserved in 75-million-year-old dinosaur specimens.* S.Bertazzo and others, Nature Communications 6, Article no. 7352, 2015.
[99] *On the Origin of Species*, 1st edition. C.Darwin, John Murray, London, 1859, chapter 6, p.171.

God, Science and the Bible

argument can hardly be sustained today. Since Darwin's day not millions but billions of fossils have been recovered from all over the world. A spokesman for London's Natural History Museum wrote that *'in terms of the number of individual fossils there are probably countless billions. Most large Natural History Museums will have a collection of several million.'*[100] Yet still, in spite of all these fossil finds, there is no evidence of gradual change from one species to another as Darwin's hypothesis predicted.[101] A proper scientific theory must be supported by evidence, not mere conjecture!

It is true that from time to time there is found a fossil of something new that combines some features of two other known life forms. It is often immediately hailed in the media as 'a missing link', or sometimes even '*the* missing link' as though only two transitional stages were needed to change from one form to the other. But the only thing that a new kind of fossil proves is that something once lived that is not known to live today. It doesn't prove that one of the things it resembles evolved into the other one, or even in which direction the supposed evolution went. That is well illustrated by the fossil of a deinonychus discovered in 1969, which was identified as a bird-like dinosaur and a possible ancestor of birds, until the discovery in China of flying ancestors changed it into a bird that had lost the ability to fly.[102] So instead of being a dinosaur that was learning to fly it became a bird that had forgotten how to do it!

For another thing, although popular science gives the impression that fossils consist mainly of creatures like boring little ammonites or animals and plants that are now extinct, the vast majority are of the very same life forms as those that exist today. Stromatolites, the 'oldest' fossils on earth and supposedly 3.5 billion years old, are still being formed in lagoons in Australasia and are virtually identical.[103]

---

[100] Graeme Lloyd, 4th May 2008.
http://www.askabiologist.org.uk/answers/viewtopic.php?id=1408, viewed October 2016.

[101] I think that nowadays, Darwin might have written 'genus' rather than 'species'.

[102] The change of status of the deinonychus is described on a plaque displaying the fossil at an exhibition at the Royal Ontario Museum in 2005. (*Feathered Dinosaurs*, The Dinosaur Museum, Blanding, UT, USA.)

[103] *Evolution's Achilles' Heels*. Ed. R.Carter, Creation Book Publishers, 2014, p. 139.

The Fossil Record

Tassel ferns, Wollemi pines, fig trees, sponges, seaweed, mussels, jellyfish, starfish, horseshoe crabs (supposedly 445 million years old[104]), the amazing nautilus, coelacanths, herrings, mackerel, lobsters, crayfish, sharks, scorpions, silverfish, spiders, cockroaches, dragonflies, frogs, tortoises, musk oxen, antelopes, reindeer, tigers, Arctic foxes, bears and horses are all fossilized examples of creatures that are alive and well today.[105,106,107] How were they all buried alive in sedimentary rocks if not by a worldwide flood?

> *Deposits found in Lincoln County, Wyoming, furnish some of the most perfect specimens of fossil fish and plants in the world... Other than fish, palm leaves from 6 to 8 feet in length and from 3 to 4 feet wide have been uncovered... an alligator was found. Several garpike, ranging in size from 4 to 6 feet have been disentombed, as have birds of about the size of the domestic chicken and resembling the snipe or plover in general conformation. In addition, specimens of sunfish, rasp-tongues, deep sea bass, chubs, pickerel and herring have been found, not to mention mollusca, crustaceans, birds, turtles, mammals and many varieties of insects.*[108]

Generally, the only difference between a fossil and its living equivalent today is that sometimes the fossilized ancestor was much larger. The true scientific evidence of the fossil record is that species have remained unchanged ever since their earliest forms.

Thus the evidence of the fossil record is that species are not evolving. Why should they? If a horseshoe crab has really remained perfectly adapted to its environment for 445 million years without succumbing to any newly evolved predators, why would it ever want to change into something else? The evidence of the fossil record is entirely consistent with the repeated refrain in Genesis chapter 1, that

---

[104] Science Daily, 8 February, 2008.
[105] *Evolution's Achilles' Heels*. Ed. R.Carter, Creation Book Publishers, 2014, chapter 4.
[106] *The World of Living Fossils*. Creation Research, Australia, 2003. (A DVD that shows photos of fossils and their living counterparts side by side.)
[107] The *Quaternary Era, Volume II*. Edward Arnold Co., London, 1957, p.650.
[108] *Fishing for Fossils*. Compressed Air Magazine, March 1958, volume 63, p.24.

God, Science and the Bible

God created vegetation, fruit trees, sea creatures, winged birds, beasts, cattle and insects, each *according to their kinds*. Apart from variations within each kind (contrast an Irish wolfhound with a chihuahua) the fossil *evidence* is that flora and fauna have remained unchanged according to their kinds ever since.

So why believe in evolution?

In Chapter 2, I argued on logical grounds that the theory of evolution can't be true. Here, I have shown that it's not supported by scientific evidence either. So why are so many scientists convinced that it *is* true? Some ardent advocates of evolution are chiefly motivated by a hatred of God or the very idea of God. But for many of them it's simply because they cannot believe in the idea of supernatural creation, and evolution is the only other way they can explain the existence of life as we know it. Some of them have openly admitted this. Another David Watson, who until 1951 was Professor of Zoology and Comparative Anatomy at University College, London, wrote that the theory of evolution is *'a theory universally accepted not because it can be proved by logically coherent evidence to be true but because the only alternative, special creation, is clearly incredible.'*[109]

Even this candid admission that the theory of evolution is not supported by evidence contained lies. The theory of evolution is not universally accepted, and it is incredible only to those who refuse to believe in God.

---

[109] *Adaptation.* D.M.S.Watson, Nature, Vol. 124, 10 August 1929, p.233. The quotation and reference are given in the Wikipedia entry on D.M.S.Watson.

8. The Ages of Rocks and Trees

Radioactive dating

According to the Hebrew 'Masoretic' text, on which virtually all translations of the Old Testament are based, the Flood occurred around 2300 BC and the world is currently around 6000 years old. On the other hand, radioactive dating techniques suggest that the earth's rocks are up to 4 billion years old. One or the other is wrong!

The age of rocks is determined using radioactive chemical elements. A radioactive element emits radiation in the form of atomic particles, and in doing so it gradually changes into another element. The rates at which the various radioactive elements change into other elements can be measured. Uranium, for example, very slowly turns into lead. A given weight of uranium will lose half its weight in 4.46 billion years. (I did say it changed very slowly!) The figure of 4.46 billion years is called its half-life. So if a rock has 1 gm of uranium in it when it is first formed, then 4.46 billion years later it will have only 0.5 gm of uranium in it, but there will be perhaps 0.5 gm of lead as well. (I don't know whether you get exactly 0.5 gm of lead from 0.5 gm of uranium, but you get the idea.)

From the measured proportions of uranium and lead in a rock it is therefore possible to calculate how long the uranium has been there and hence how old the rock is. For example, if there are equal amounts of uranium and lead then half the uranium must have turned into lead so the rock must be 4.46 billion years old, its half-life.

Behold, I make all things old!

When I learned how radioactive dating worked my first thought was, "How does a geologist know that there wasn't already some lead in the rock to start with?" Geologists are aware of this and other difficulties, so they try to get over them by various means.[110,111] However, if God made everything supernaturally then the entire basis of radiometric dating falls apart. God could have created rocks having radioactive elements and the stable elements into which they decay in any proportion he liked.

When I had my house extension built, I specified used tiles to match the existing ones. Anyone looking at the extension would assume it had been built at the same time as the main house, not 50 years later. There could be various reasons why God might have made 'mature' rocks rather than brand new ones. When he made Adam and Eve he could not make two newborn babies and leave them to fend for themselves: he had to make a mature man and woman. When he made fruit trees he could not make tiny first-year saplings or Adam and Eve would have had no fruit to eat for several years: he had to make mature fruit trees. When he made the stars he could not make 'new' ones which had only just started to shine, or Adam and Eve would have died before they could see the more distant ones: he had to make 'mature' stars that had apparently been shining for a long time. So when he made rocks, it might have been equally necessary for him to make mature rocks that had every appearance of age, rather than brand new ones. What scientific law states that he had to make a rock with uranium in it but no lead, or one with samarium in it but no neodymium, or one with rubidium in it but no strontium?

In Chapter 2, I explained why the physical universe and terrestrial life could have come into existence only supernaturally. If the earth's rocks were created supernaturally then radioactive dating will be unable to determine their age, because the proportions of radioactive elements and non-radioactive elements that were in them when they were created will be unknown. And since it is impossible to prove from any observations or measurements whether this natural earth was created naturally or supernaturally, it is impossible to prove from measurements of radioactivity whether rocks really are old or not.

---

[110] *Nuclear Processes in Geologic Settings: Interpretation of lead isotope abundances.* R.D.Russell, National Academy of Science, National Research Council publication 400, 1956, pp.68-78.

[111] *Nuclear Processes in Geologic Settings: Leakage of uranium and lead and the measurement of geological time.* F.E.Wickman, National Academy of Science, National Research Council publication 400, 1956, pp.62-67.

The Ages of Rocks and Trees

The apparent ages of rocks determined by radioactive dating are no proof that the earth is a day older than the Bible implies.

Trees older than the earth?

The oldest living trees are believed to be around 5000 years old. According to the Bible, this means these bristlecone pine trees must have lived through the Flood, which seems most unlikely. What is not so well known is that the remains of some dead oak trees found in Germany and Switzerland are believed to be more than 13,000 years old. If that is true, then according to the Bible they must have been growing before the creation of the world! Once again we have a conflict between the Bible and scientists, this time with scientists who specialize in dendrochronology.

Dendrochronology

The main method used to determine the age of a tree is to count the number of growth rings in the trunk. Each year the bark of a tree creates a ring of new wood around its trunk, and since the wood grown in springtime is lighter in colour than the slower-grown autumn wood, the annual rings can be identified and counted. You've probably seen them in the stump of a tree that has been felled. So in general, the number of rings is equal to the number of years that the tree has lived. Tree surgeons can discover the number of rings in a living tree by twisting a hollow auger called an increment borer into its trunk and extracting a 4 mm or 5 mm diameter rod of timber called a core sample. The sample displays a cross section of the growth rings without killing the tree.

    Counting the growth rings does sound like a simple and foolproof method to find out how old a tree is, or how old it was when it died. So is it really possible that the tree scientists who dated the pine and oak trees could have been totally mistaken?

Bristlecone pine rings

Let's begin with the bristlecone pine trees. These apparently long-lived trees grow in the higher mountains of the south-western USA. According to researchers Ed Schulman and Tom Harlan a tree named 'Methuselah' living in the White Mountains of Colorado was 4845 years old in 2012 and another unnamed tree was 5062 years old.[112] The Wikipedia entry on 'Pinus longaeva' says that that age of the Methuselah tree was measured on an annual ring count using an increment borer. However, determining Methuselah's age was not nearly as simple as that. Schulman and Harlan themselves say, 'Ring-counted ages are derived by simple ring counts and may contain errors in age due to missing or false rings, suppressed areas, or other tree-ring anomalies'. Therefore, in the case of these very old trees, the pattern of rings was compared with the patterns from similar adjacent trees in order to build up a more certain picture, at least back to the early years of the adjacent younger trees.

Counting the rings of the older bristlecone pine trees is particularly difficult because the bark (which is what produces the rings) doesn't extend all around the trunk. It twists in a spiral up the tree, and in the oldest specimens only a narrow strip of living tissue connects the roots to a handful of live branches. A further difficulty is that with an estimated 5000 rings, each ring is only on average 0.36 mm wide, making reliable identification and cross-matching even harder. Some are so thin that a microscope is needed to distinguish one from another.[113]

A paradox and its explanation

One further factor brings into question the whole basis of ring counting in the case of ancient bristlecone pines. Normally one would expect a tree planted in good soil with plenty of rain and warmth to be healthier and to live longer than a less favoured tree of the same species. In fact the apparently oldest bristlecone pine trees grow in the worst imaginable conditions, high up on cold, dry and windy mountain slopes. In the White Mountains the annual precipitation of only 250 mm falls mostly as snow, and in the summer the air is said to be the driest on earth. Worse still, there is so little soil that some trees grow out of little more than a crack in the rocks. As a result, what rain there is soon evaporates or drains away.

---

[112] *Rocky Mountain Tree Ring Research.* http://www.rmtrr.org/oldlist.htm. Viewed June 2023.
[113] *Longevity under adversity in conifers.* E.Schulman, Science 119:398, 1954.

Yet these particular bristlecone pines have so many rings that they appear to live about ten times longer than bristlecone pines which grow in comparatively good conditions![114] Even on the White Mountains themselves, the trees on north-facing slopes appear to live twice as long as those on south-facing slopes.[115] Why should this be?

The explanation is given in a *Tree-Ring Bulletin*, published way back in 1938.[116] This is a study of 'false annual rings' in Monterey pine, another species of pine and nowadays known as radiata pine. Schulman wrote: '*A double ring or multiple ring is due to the interruption of the normal course of growth of a season... such a ring is known as a false annual ring... False rings climatic in origin are those most commonly met with... Not infrequently climatic vicissitudes will cause not one but several false rings of this type to occur.*' In his 600-page book *The Genus Pinus*, Mirov states, '*Apparently a semblance of annual rings is formed after every rather infrequent cloudburst.*'[117]

It therefore seems certain that the bristlecone pines which grow in extremely arid conditions have developed a method of surviving by growing a little each time some moisture becomes available and then stopping until some more comes along. To my mind this is confirmed by the fact that in the central area of a stand of bristlecone pine trees, where growing conditions are the best, the trees do not have more than several hundred rings, whereas at the margins of the stand,[118] where the soil thins and growing conditions become progressively poorer, trees with many more rings are found.[119]

A stand of similar trees normally starts with one tree, grown perhaps from a cone or seed dropped by an animal or bird. Over the years it produces other trees immediately around it, and then these

---

[114] *Evidence for multiple ring growth per year in Bristlecone Pines*. M.Matthews, www.creation.com/bristlecone-pines. Viewed June 2023.

[115] *Ancient Trees: Trees that Live for a Thousand Years*. A.Lewington & E.Parker, Collins & Brown Ltd, 1999,p.37. (This book was updated and republished by Anna Lewington in 2012.)

[116] *Classification of False Annual Rings in Monterey Pine*. E.Schulman, Tree-Ring Society, Tree-Ring Bulletin 4(3):4-7, 1938.

[117] *The Genus Pinus*. N.T.Mirov, Ronald Press Co., New York, 1967.

[118] A stand of trees is a group of trees sufficiently uniform in every aspect to distinguish it from adjacent groups.

[119] *Environment in Relation to Age of Bristlecone Pines*. V.C.LaMarche, Ecology 50(1), 1969, pp.56-57.

produce further trees, working progressively outwards. Thus, in a naturally grown stand of trees, the ones on the outside are the youngest ones, not the oldest ones as ring counts on Bristlecone pines suggests they are.

The trees growing at the margins of typical stand of Bristlecone pines have more growth rings, not because they are older, but simply because the soil is poorer so they are starved for water and they grow rings each time some water becomes available.

Schulman says that it is normally possible to distinguish such false rings from true annual ones, but in some cases where there is a double ring (growth in the spring and the autumn only) the two rings appear identical. Glock and colleagues demonstrated that in dry climates the band of darker wood that separates a false ring from the next one could have outer boundaries that are every bit as distinct as the outer boundaries of a true annual ring.[120] Therefore 'false rings' can be indistinguishable from 'true' annual rings. The difficulty is multiplied in the case of the bristlecone pines that have several thousand rings, for as well as being incomplete these rings are necessarily extremely thin. Since the ring pattern in similar trees in similar climatic conditions is likely to be similar, attempting to identify false rings by cross-matching the patterns can hardly be relied upon to identify false rings. *'The fact that the thin, entire growth layers or lenses match from one tree to another does not prove their annual character,'* Glock concluded.

It is clear that bristlecone pine trees in the harshest environmental conditions grow multiple rings each year that cannot always be distinguished from annual rings. The result is that the ages of these trees cannot be determined by ring counting even with cross-matching, and attempting to do so produces apparent ages far greater than their true ages.[121] They are not 5000 years old!

---

[120] *Classification and multiplicity of growth layers in the branches of trees.* W.S.Glock and others, Smithsonian Miscellaneous Collections 140:1, 1960, p.275.

[121] For a critique of evidence in support of 5000 year ages see *Evidence for multiple ring growth per year in Bristlecone Pines* by M.Matthews, http://creation.com/evidence-for-multiple-ring-growth-per-year-in-bristlecone-pines. Viewed June 2023.

Even more ancient oaks?

The oak trees that were supposed to have been alive 13,000 years ago in parts of Germany and Switzerland are a different case. Instead of talking about the longevity of living trees we are talking about pieces of dead trees and deciding when the trees that they came from were alive. The purpose of such research is to build up a database of dated growth rings so that measurements of their carbon content can be used to determine the C_{14} level in the atmosphere each year as far back as possible. An accurate knowledge of the historical levels of C_{14} is necessary to support the accuracy of C_{14} dating.[122,123]

None of the original trees is likely to have lived for more than 1000 years, so the method involves chaining together pieces of dead trees of successively older origin by attempting to match overlapping sections of their growth rings. The width of a growth ring depends to a large extent on the weather that year. In very dry years the tree will not grow so much and the growth ring will be narrower. So over the years, there will be a pattern of thin, medium or wide growth rings that is similar in each tree, and the pattern of the first few years of a younger tree will be similar to the pattern of the last few years of an older tree that preceded it if their years of growth overlap. Provided that a continuous chain of overlapping dates can be found it is possible to continue going back in time, so long as pieces of dead wood of ages that overlap still survive and can be found. Figure 2 illustrates how pieces of wood from three different trees might be chained together like this.

---

[122] *Atmospheric 14C variations derived from tree rings during the early Younger Dryas.* Q.Hua and others, Quaternary Science Reviews 28(25–26): 2982–90, 2009.

[123] *Lateglacial environmental variability from Swiss tree rings.* M.Schaub and others, Quaternary Science Reviews 27(1–2): pp.29–41, 2008.

God, Science and the Bible

Figure 2: Growth ring chaining

The procedure seems straightforward, but it involves serious difficulties. The first is that sequences of growth rings are not unique, especially over several thousand years, and two similar sequences might occur several centuries apart. Even in the same period, the patterns of growth rings are not identical on every tree. So judgement is required as to whether or not a pattern from one tree matches one from another, and whether it is the only possible position over a period of several thousand years that will produce such a match.

By way of illustrating this, see if you can decide which of the four possible alignments of the large fragment from one tree and the small fragment from another tree is correct in Figure 3. Remember that even patterns from the same years might not match each other exactly.

Figure 3: Growth ring matching (1)

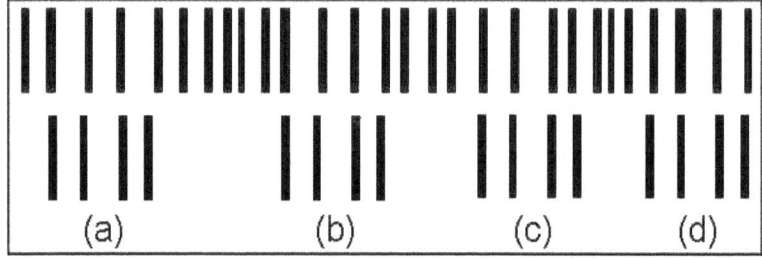

In fact none of them is right! In Figure 4, both specimens are from the same two trees as in Figure 3 except that a longer specimen from the first tree now has another 9 annual growth rings on its right-hand end. This allows an almost perfect match to be found with the specimen from the second tree.

In practice, a specimen with only four annual rings would not be used to create a link in the chain: the short specimen in the diagrams is for explanatory purposes only.

Figure 4: Growth ring matching (2)

One demonstration of the uncertainties inherent in this procedure is that a chronology from Somerset in South West England and another early but detailed one from southern Germany were both 'remeasured' when a contradictory one was published by Queen's University in Belfast, Northern Ireland, even though the authors of at least the German study had previously been confident of its accuracy.[124]

Ring sequencing and C_{14} dating

Beyond the uncertainties regarding matching, there is a still more serious problem with such databases when they go too far back in time. In order to make use of a piece of wood its approximate age is first determined using carbon 14 dating. An attempt is then made to match the pattern of growth rings in it with a pattern in the chain of specimens of a similar age that has already been established. If more than one good match is found, the one that is chosen will usually be the one from a date that best coincides with the C_{14} date of the new specimen.

But while C_{14} dating may be fine for dates back to the pharaohs in 2625 BC it becomes wildly unreliable in the years immediately after

---

[124] *A Test of Time*. D.Rohl, Arrow Books, London, Appendix C, 1996.

the flood around 2300 BC, as I have explained. It inevitably indicates dates far earlier than it should because the first trees to grow after the Flood would have grown up in an atmosphere that initially had very little radioactive carbon in it. So instead of chaining together older and older pieces of tree, dendrochronologists are simply chaining together pieces of tree that happen to have less and less minute quantities of C_{14} in them. After all, it is hard to believe that specimens of wood could survive for 13,000 years without rotting away or being eaten by something, whereas they might survive in suitable conditions if they were from trees that had started to grow soon after 2300 BC and died 500 years later.

Of course, once a database of tree rings supposedly going back 13,000 years or more has been established, the tree rings can be used to 'prove' the reliability of radiocarbon dating, because C_{14} measurement of the oldest specimens in the chain will indeed indicate ages of 13,000 years or more! It's not only tree rings that are circular: the argument proving their old age is circular too!

9. The Bible as the Word of God

Is the Bible truly the word of God?

Simply believing in God's existence doesn't get us very far. It's like laying the foundation for a house without building anything on it. What use is a belief in God if we don't build our lives upon it? You and I are not accidents: God made us for a purpose, one that will continue forever. He wants us to know him. He wants us to know what he is like, to know what he has done, to know what he intends to do, and most importantly to know what he wants us to do. And because he can do anything he has arranged to have all this written down for us. The Bible, above all other books, tells us the truth about God and his plans for the world and for you and me. It not only tells us that he created the world, but it explains why so much has gone wrong with it and provides a solution in which you and I can take part. So the final questions we must now address are these: is the Bible truly the word of God, and if it is, what difference will it make to us?

Where did the Bible come from?

Where did the Holy Bible come from? Although the Jewish race began with one man—Abraham—Jews would probably regard the birthday of their nation as the day when nearly 700,000 Hebrew men escaped from Egypt, together with their wives, children and animals. (Numbers 1.44-47)[125] The dramatic moment when Moses opened an escape route for them through the sea by striking it with his staff at God's command authenticated Moses as a leader who was genuinely in touch with God. (I love the story of the primary school teacher somewhere in the old Soviet Union who told her class that the sea

---

[125] For a discussion of the external historical evidence for the Exodus story see chapter 10 of *The Bible as History: Second Revised Edition*. W.Keller & J.Rohork, Harper Collins, 2015.

was really only a few inches deep, so it wasn't a miracle at all. One small girl put her hand up and asked, "Did God really drown all Pharaoh's soldiers and horses in only a few inches of water? Wasn't he clever!")

During the 40 years encamped in the wilderness that followed, Moses spent long hours in conversation with God. Two important facts are recorded. One, that 'the Lord used to speak to Moses face to face, as a man speaks to his friend' (Exodus 33.11); and two, that God frequently told Moses to write down what he had said to him. (Exodus 17.14, 24.4, 34.27,28; Deuteronomy 31.9) Moses kept a log of their travels (Numbers 33.2) and he even wrote a song. (Deuteronomy 31.22) (No, it wasn't, 'Go down, Moses.' Pharaoh had already let God's people go!)

Moses had been educated in the Egyptian royal palace and was 'mighty in his words' (Acts 7.22), so clearly God had prepared him for his role as the nation's first archivist, as well as its lawgiver and major prophet. Jewish oral tradition says that Moses was in fact the author of the first five books of the Bible, from Genesis to Deuteronomy. He had 40 years in the wilderness to do it, so this was perfectly possible. Even if he wasn't directly responsible for every word of those books, he could still have been the author of the material used by later scribes to write the rest. But one thing seems certain to me. If he was conversing face to face with the Lord for 40 years, he would have asked the Lord among other things how he made the world. That would explain how we have an account in Genesis of something that happened before there were any human observers to record it.[126]

During succeeding centuries, God called other men and women to spend time in his presence in order to hear and proclaim his words to the nation. The prophets were almost always reluctant to take on this role, for two reasons. In Deuteronomy 18.20-22 God said, *"The prophet who presumes to speak a word in my name which I have not commanded him to speak... that same prophet shall die."* And when the people asked,

---

[126] A second source of information about how God created the world would have been Adam, with whom the Lord also conversed face to face. Adam would certainly have asked, "Where did I come from?" I believe that he passed down to his descendants what he was told, which accounts for the second version of the creation story in Genesis that focusses more on the creation of man.

"How may we know the word which the Lord has not spoken?" the reply was, *"If the word does not come to pass or come true, that is a word which the Lord has not spoken."* Astrologers like the Astro Twins, Susan Miller, Chani Nicholas and Debbie Frank should be thankful they didn't live in those days! Secondly, the prophets almost invariably suffered abuse or even death at the hands of rebellious kings and people who didn't like hearing the truth. (Matthew 23.34,35) Jeremiah was thrown down a well, Daniel was thrown to the lions, and Zacharias was stoned to death in the temple court. All this tells me that the relatively few men and women of God who accepted God's call to be a prophet and whose words survive in the Bible must have been very special people indeed, whose words can be trusted.

The verdict of Jesus

For Christians, the definitive answer to the question "Is the Bible truly the word of God?" is found in Jesus Christ. As the author of the New Testament letter to the Hebrews wrote, *'In many and various ways God spoke of old to our fathers by the prophets; but in these last days he has spoken to us by a Son.'* (Hebrews 1.1,2) As we've seen, Jesus was indeed the Son of God. Among other things he came to tell us the truth about God and his purposes in creating the world. If we therefore believe that Jesus is 'the way, and the truth, and the life' as he claimed to be (John 14.6) then we have no alternative but to believe that the things he said were true. At one point he said, *"I have not spoken on my own authority; the Father who sent me has himself given me commandment what to say and what to speak. …What I say, therefore, I say as the Father has bidden me."* (John 12.49,50)

So what did Jesus himself say about the scriptures? When Jesus spoke about the scriptures, he was of course speaking about what Christians call the Old Testament, what Jews call the Tanakh, and what Muslims call The Book. We'll have to consider the New Testament separately, but what Jesus said about the Old Testament leaves us in no doubt that he believed it to be the true word of God.

"…scripture cannot be broken," he said. (John 10.35)

"Man shall not live by bread alone, but by every word that proceeds from the mouth of God." (Matthew 4.4) Jesus was quoting from the book of Deuteronomy, one of the first five books in the Old Testament.

"For truly, I say to you, till heaven and earth pass away, not an iota, not a dot, will pass from the law until all is accomplished." (Matthew 5.18) ('The law' referred to all the first five books of the Old Testament. Jesus was saying that even the tiniest part of each individual letter must come true.)

"Have you not read that he who made them from the beginning made them male and female…" (Matthew 19.4—a reference to the account of creation in Genesis.)

'He said to them, "For your hardness of heart Moses allowed you to divorce your wives, but from the beginning it was not so."' (Matthew 19.8—a reference to the period immediately after creation before Adam and Eve's sin hardened the hearts of humanity.)

"…that upon you may come all the righteous blood shed on earth, from the blood of innocent Abel to the blood of Zechariah the son of Barachiah, whom you murdered between the sanctuary and the altar." (Matthew 23:35—a reference to Adam's and Eve's son Abel as the first person ever to be murdered, by his brother!)

"As it was in the days of Noah, so will it be in the days of the Son of man. They ate, they drank, they married, they were given in marriage, until the day when Noah entered the ark, and the flood came and destroyed them all." (Luke 17.26,27—a reference to the flood as a historical event.)

"For as Jonah was three days and three nights in the belly of the whale…" (Matthew 12.40—a belief in the literal truth of the Jonah story. The Greek word means 'sea monster', not whale.)

"…everything written about me in the law of Moses and the prophets and the psalms must be fulfilled." (Luke 24.44—a belief in every Old Testament prophecy that pointed to himself.)

I think the most amazing illustration of Jesus's belief in the Old Testament scriptures and his commitment to live by them is what happened in the darkness of the night that he was arrested. With three of his disciples on watch close by, he was pleading with his heavenly father for strength to face the coming ordeal of crucifixion. Suddenly lights appeared, and a huge mob armed with swords and clubs surrounded him. Peter, loyal to the point of madness, drew his sword and started to attack them. Jesus rebuked him. *"Put your sword back into its place; for all who take the sword will perish by the sword. Do you think that I cannot appeal to my Father, and he will at once send me more than twelve legions of angels? But how then should the scriptures be fulfilled, that it must be so? …all this has taken place, that the scriptures of the prophets might be fulfilled."* (Matthew 26.52-56) In the mind of Jesus, everything that the prophets said was true, therefore everything that they foretold had to be fulfilled at its appointed time, even including his death. Rewriting the script was not an option.

In accordance with Jesus's belief in the truth of the scriptures, he paid minute attention to their precise wording. To prove that there is life after death, he asked, *"...have you not read in the book of Moses, in the passage about the bush, how God said to him, 'I am the God of Abraham, and the God of Isaac, and the God of Jacob'? He is not God of the dead, but of the living..."* (Mark 12.26,27) His argument was that because God said 'I am' with the verb in the present tense and not 'I was', Abraham, Isaac and Jacob must still have been alive.

Similarly Jesus cited verse 1 of King David's Psalm 110, *'The Lord says to my lord'*, to prove that David regarded the Messiah as someone who would be far greater than he himself was—'my lord'. Such close attention to the detail of the words in the scriptures is typical of orthodox Jewish rabbis even today.

Paul would later write, *'...we have the mind of Christ.'* (1 Corinthians 2.16) To have the mind of Jesus Christ is to believe as Jesus did that what was originally written in the Old Testament is true, whatever today's unbelieving world may think. *'All scripture is inspired by God...'* Paul declared (2 Timothy 3.16), and the other New Testament writers were in full agreement with him.

Dependable or distorted?

Inevitably some minor changes to the original text may have crept into the Old Testament through the process of copying manuscripts by hand, but the scribes held their scriptures in such high regard that they were incredibly careful to copy them accurately. James McClinton[127] tells us that one method they employed to avoid mistakes was to use 'checksums' similar to those used by modern computer programmers. For the purposes of counting, each letter in the Hebrew alphabet also has a numerical value. For example, Aleph = 1, Beit = 2, and further on Nun = 50 and Kuf = 100. When they made a copy of the scriptures, the scribes would add the values of all the letters in each row of the original document and compare them

---

[127] *Quid Pro Quirk.* J.McClinton, WestBow Press, 2014.

God, Science and the Bible

with the corresponding sums in the copied document to check that the two documents were identical. The Dead Sea Scrolls, discovered between 1946 and 1956, included every book of the Old Testament except one, yet although they were written more than a thousand years *before* the currently accepted Hebrew text there are no significant differences between them.

Admittedly, when the original Hebrew is translated into other languages, the translations may not always accurately represent the original meaning. It may sometimes be necessary to compare different translations or even to go back to the original Hebrew (or Greek in the case of the New Testament) in order to be certain of the original meaning.

Literal or legendary?

While the Bible is true, not every word of it is intended to be taken literally. It includes metaphors, parables and other figures of speech. David didn't literally mean that God was a rock (Psalm 28.1), neither did the lover in the Song of Solomon really want his sweetheart's breasts to be clusters of grapes! (Song of Solomon 7.8) The prophet Nathan told King David a story about a rich man who stole a poor man's only lamb in order to provide a meal for his guest, in order to force the king to realize how badly he had behaved in his own treatment of a subject. Clearly this was a parable that Nathan had made up for the occasion. (A parable is an earthly story with a heavenly meaning.) Nevertheless it is obvious to any unbiased reader that the first five books of the Bible and the historical books that follow them were intended to be understood literally, and that is certainly how Jesus understood them.

When there is doubt, how can we tell if a passage should be taken literally? John Wesley, the founder of Methodism in the eighteenth century, wrote, '*It is a stated rule in interpreting Scripture never to depart from the plain, literal sense, unless it implies an absurdity.*'[128] He meant that we should always understand a word or a sentence to mean what it plainly says, so long as it makes sense to do so.

---

[128] *Sermon 74: Of the Church.* J.Wesley, *Sermons on Several Occasions*, Wesleyan Conference Office, London, 1876. Paragraph 12.

The Bible as the Word of God

In the case of the Bible's account of a six-day creation in the first chapter of Genesis, interpreting it literally is absurd only if God doesn't exist or if he never does anything supernaturally. But if the world was created supernaturally—and I've argued in Chapter 2 that it could not have been created in any other way—then God could have done it in any order and in any period of time he chose. In that case there is nothing absurd about interpreting the account of creation in the book of Genesis literally, therefore by Wesley's rule that is how it should be interpreted and understood.

In particular, the first chapter of Genesis is not a poem as some Bible teachers claim. Hebrew poetry had its own special style. It did not have lines that rhyme as traditional English poetry has, nor did it have an obvious metre as traditional hymns have. Hebrew poetry was usually in the form of couplets that either said the same thing in different ways, or provided two contrasting aspects of the same truth. In this form, the cantor, or worship leader, could say the first part of each couplet, and the congregation could respond with the second part. For example, Psalm 100 begins:

Make a joyful noise to the Lord, all the lands!
Serve the Lord with gladness! Come into his presence with singing!
Know that the Lord is God!
It is he that made us, and we are his; we are his people, and the sheep of his pasture.
Enter his gates with thanksgiving, and his courts with praise!
Give thanks to him, bless his name!

The first chapter of Genesis is nothing like that. But even if it were a poem, it could still be literally true. Another good example of Hebrew poetry is the song of celebration that Moses and his people sang after escaping from Egypt (Exodus 15.1-18). Every word of that was literally true.

The reliability of the New Testament

What about the New Testament? As I have already said, much of it was written by Jesus's own early disciples or their close associates, Matthew, Mark, Luke, John and Peter. There is even a letter written by James, the half-brother of Jesus. Most of the letters in the New Testament were written by Paul. He was not one of the original disciples, but a highly trained Jewish rabbi. The risen Lord Jesus appeared to him and personally appointed him as a preacher and teacher to the non-Jewish world. In a curious comment about Paul's letters, Peter wrote, '*So also our beloved brother Paul wrote to you according to the wisdom given him, speaking of* [the end of the age] *as he does in all his letters. There are some things in them hard to understand, which the ignorant and unstable twist to their own destruction, as they do the other scriptures.*' (2 Peter 3.15,16) Peter, the ex-fisherman, evidently struggled at times to follow some of Paul's learned arguments, nevertheless he referred to Paul's letters as among 'the other scriptures', placing them on a par with the Old Testament.

The opening verses of Luke's gospel story give us an idea of Luke's desire to report only the truth. '*Inasmuch as many have undertaken to compile a narrative of the things which have been accomplished among us, just as they were delivered to us by those who from the beginning were eyewitnesses and ministers of the word, it seemed good to me also, having followed all things closely for some time past, to write an orderly account for you, most excellent Theophilus, that you many know the truth concerning the things of which you have been informed.*' (Luke 1.1-4)

These New Testament authors were well aware of the difference between truth and falsehood. Peter wrote, '*For we did not follow cleverly devised myths when we made known to you the power and coming of our Lord Jesus Christ, but we were eyewitnesses of his majesty. For when he received honour and glory from God the Father, the voice was borne to him by the Majestic Glory, "This is my beloved Son, with whom I am well pleased," we heard this voice borne from heaven, for we were with him on the holy mountain.*' (2 Peter 1.16-18)

Furthermore, Jesus promised his followers special help in recording his teaching and actions after he left them. *"...the Counsellor, the Holy Spirit, whom the Father will send in my name, he will teach you all things, and bring to your remembrance all that I have said to you."* (John 14.26) *"When the Spirit of truth comes, he will guide you into all the truth..."* (John 16.13) Therefore if Jesus was the Son of God—and his resurrection is the proof of that—then the general truth of the New Testament cannot be in doubt.

It's true that the four Gospel writers don't always report the teachings of Jesus or events in exactly the same way, but this only reflects the differences that always occur when witnesses to a real event report what they have seen and heard from different perspectives. After all, if all four Gospels were identical it would be obvious that three of the writers had simply copied the fourth one, who might then have made it all up. Isn't that what frequently happens on the Internet today?

As in the Old Testament, not everything in the New Testament is intended to be taken literally. Jesus's teaching in particular includes many parables (e.g. the parable of the prodigal son in Luke chapter 15). There are metaphors ('the Lamb of God' in John chapter 1—Jesus was not really a lamb), figures of speech ('a thorn in the flesh' in 2 Corinthians chapter 12), and symbolical visions (the great harlot in Revelation chapter 17). But when a passage is meant to be understood literally it is usually obvious. We may sometimes need the Holy Spirit's help to separate literal truth from other kinds of truth, but we can have that help if our minds and hearts are open to the Spirit.

Admittedly, two matters that need some explanation are why Jesus told his first disciples that he would return during their lifetime, and how a merciful God can consign people to everlasting torment in hell, if indeed he will. I haver answered these two questions in my book *The Date of Christ's Return*.

But back to essentials. The Lord himself wants to speak to us through the words that his chosen apostles, prophets and teachers have recorded for us. That is why he chose and trained them. Our response to what he says through them will determine our eternal destiny, and that includes yours! As John wrote near the end of his Gospel, '...*these things are written that you may believe that Jesus is the Christ, the Son of God, and that believing you may have life in his name.*' (John 20.31) Revelation 21.5 says, "...*these words are trustworthy and true.*" That is how Jesus regarded the Old Testament, and it's how he wants us to regard the New Testament too. The New Testament is a unique document written by people whom the Lord himself equipped, appointed, inspired and trusted to convey his message of salvation to you and me.

God, Science and the Bible

Some amazing prophecies in the Old Testament

One New Year's Day on BBC Radio 4, a lady who claimed to be a clairvoyant made six predictions of things that would happen in the coming year. They covered politics, sport and a couple of celebrities. I made a note of her predictions to see if they would come true. Not one of them did. In two cases the exact opposite happened! So when we look at the prophecies made in the Old Testament and see how amazingly they were fulfilled, it is hard to come to any other conclusion than that God really did tell these ancient prophets what to say, and that they really did know what the future held, both for times now past, and for the future still to come concerning Christ's return as king and the creation of a new earth. Here are some of those prophecies for times now past and how they were fulfilled.

Genesis 12.1,2 says, *'Now the Lord said to Abram, "…I will make of you a great nation, and I will bless you, and make your name great, so that you will be a blessing."* Nowadays, almost everyone has heard of Abraham: his name is certainly great. According to the Forbes' Billionaires List in 2013, 24 out of the 100 richest men in the world were Jews—or if not Jews then they were at least Jew*ish*, as the entertainer Sammy Davis Junior once described himself. Since Jewish men make up only 0.1% of the world's population, i.e. 1 out of every 1000, the fact that 24 out of the 100 wealthiest men are Jews is an astonishing fulfilment of God's promise to bless Abraham and his descendants.

God also promised that he would make Abraham and his descendants a blessing. 22% of all Nobel Prizes in all fields have been awarded to a people group who make up only one quarter of one percent of the world's population![129] Above all, the nation of Israel has blessed the world mightily through its revelation of God and by giving birth to Jesus Christ.

Abraham's first son, Ishmael, was the ancestor of the Arab race. An angel told Ishmael's mother, Hagar, *"He shall be a wild ass of a man, his hand against every man and every man's hand against him; and he shall dwell*

---

[129] Jewish people (including male and female persons of half-or three-quarters-Jewish ancestry) currently make up only 0.25% of the world's population, but between 1901 and 2009 at least 179 Jewish people had been awarded a Nobel Prize, i.e. 22% of all individual recipients worldwide and 36% of all US recipients during the same period. This is totally astonishing.

over against all his kinsman." (Genesis 16.12) Today the hostility of Arabs towards the nation of Israel and the mutual hostility between Sunni and Shiite Muslim Arabs are a clear fulfilment of those words of prophecy.

There are thought to be some 300 prophecies in the Old Testament about Christ's birth, life, death and resurrection. His birth of a virgin in Bethlehem, his ministry in Galilee, his miracles of healing, his entry into Jerusalem on a donkey, his betrayal for 30 pieces of silver—these and more aspects of his life were all foretold hundreds of years earlier.

Two of the most remarkable prophecies concern his death. According to the Gospel writers and the first century Jewish historian Flavius Josephus, Jesus died by crucifixion. This was a horrible method of execution, which is first mentioned in history in 519 BC. The Encyclopaedia Britannica says that Darius I, king of Persia, crucified 3000 political opponents in Babylon. The Gospel writers tell us that at his trial, Jesus was silent in the face of the accusations made against him; he was sentenced to death illegally by Pilate and scourged; and when the Roman soldiers were nailing his hands to the cross he prayed, *"Father, forgive them; for they know not what they do."* (Luke 23.34)

Matthew tells us that the onlooking priests, scribes and elders mocked him, saying, *"He saved others; he cannot save himself... He trusts in God; let God deliver him now, if he desires him; for he said, 'I am the Son of God.'"* (Matthew 27.42,43) The four soldiers on duty divided his few clothes among themselves, but rather than cut his robe into four they threw dice for it. He would have been left wearing a loincloth at the most. He died within nine hours between two thieves who were crucified with him, and his body was buried by a wealthy man, Joseph of Arimathea, in his garden. That's a rough outline of how Jesus was sentenced and put to death.

Now some 700 years *earlier* Isaiah wrote,

> *Behold, my servant shall prosper, he shall be exalted and lifted up... his appearance was so marred, beyond human semblance... He was despised and rejected by men... He was oppressed, and he was afflicted, yet he opened not his mouth; like a lamb that is led to the slaughter, and like a sheep that before its shearers is dumb, so he opened not his mouth. By oppression and judgement he was taken away; and as for his generation,*

> who considered that he was cut off out of the land of the living, stricken for the transgression of my people? And they made his grave with the wicked and with a rich man in his death, although he had done no violence, and there was no deceit in his mouth. ...[he] was numbered with the transgressors; yet he bore the sin of many, and made intercession for the transgressors.
>
> Isaiah 52.13 to 53.12

Amazingly, Isaiah then predicted Christ's subsequent resurrection and work of salvation:

> ...when he makes himself an offering for sin, he shall see his offspring, he shall prolong his days; the will of the Lord shall prosper in his hand; he shall see the fruit of the travail of his soul and be satisfied; by his knowledge shall the righteous one, my servant, make many to be accounted righteous...
>
> Isaiah 53.10,11

Isaiah must have wondered what on earth he was talking about!

Even earlier than Isaiah, and centuries before crucifixion was known, King David foretold the manner of Christ's death in Psalm 22:

> *All who see me mock at me, they make mouths at me, they wag their heads; "He committed his cause to the Lord; let him deliver him, let him rescue him, for he delights in him!"* ... *Yea, dogs* (a derogatory Jewish term for Gentiles) *are round about me; a company of evildoers encircle me; they have pierced my hands and feet—I can count all my bones—they stare and gloat over me; they divide my garments among them, and for my raiment they cast lots.*
>
> Psalm 22.7,8,16-18

Another thousand years passed before Christ was crucified. Matthew described the scene:

> ...when [the soldiers] *had crucified him, they divided his garments among them by casting lots;* ...*the chief* priests, *with the scribes and elders, mocked him, saying, "He saved others; he cannot save himself. He*

is the King of Israel; let him come down now from the cross, and we will believe in him. He trusts in God; let God deliver him now, if he desires him; for he said, 'I am the Son of God.'"

Matthew 27.35,41-43)

Psalm 22 begins, *'My God, my God, why hast thou forsaken me?'*—the very words that Jesus cried out on the cross.

So far as I know, none of the holy books of other major religions prophesies future events in such detail. Only the Lord God, the creator of the world and the God of Israel, can foretell the future truthfully and accurately. Through the Old Testament prophets he foretold events that would happen in the life of Jesus at his first coming. Through those same Old Testament prophets and the apostles of the New Testament, and above all through his son Jesus, God has also foretold events that are yet to take place. Many of these further prophecies will be fulfilled when Christ returns. The rest will finally be fulfilled when God creates his promised new heaven and earth, when those who love him will live once more in a perfect world that is unspoilt by sin and death.[130]

---

[130] For a full explanation of these events, read my book *The Date of Christ's Return*.

God, Science and the Bible

Epilogue

Making a difference

Some things you learn make little or no difference to your life. The weather forecaster on the BBC announces, "There will be snow on the Scottish hills today." Unless you're a Scottish shepherd or you're there for a skiing holiday that weather forecast probably won't interest you in the slightest.

"The average life expectancy in the UK is now 82 years." That's certainly good news, but knowing you might live a year or two longer than you thought isn't going to make very much difference right now unless you are nearly 80!

But what about, "We have confirmed our initial diagnosis of your condition. I'm sorry to tell you that you probably have three more months to live at the most."

Now that *would* make a difference. If you still had the strength you might want spend your remaining time doing some of the things you'd always wanted to do but never got round to doing or never dared to try. Perhaps you'd visit Israel or Tahiti, or take a Mediterranean cruise, or do a skydive, or fulfil a lifelong fantasy and book a fortnight's holiday in a naturist resort! You'd want to get your affairs in order for your family; make a will if necessary; write down your wishes for your funeral. You might want to seek reconciliation with someone you'd fallen out with; forgive someone who had wronged you; or even ask forgiveness from someone whom you had wronged. You might simply want to tell someone something that you'd always wanted to say but somehow never got round to.

Your priorities would change dramatically. Some things that had previously seemed important to you—perhaps the possibility of promotion at work or the value of your savings or shares—would suddenly become totally irrelevant. On the other hand, a question that had never seriously crossed your mind might suddenly become the most important question of all. And that question might be, "If some people really will continue to live after they die in a real kind of life that fulfils all their deepest desires, what must I do to join them?"

The ultimate good news

If the Bible is true after all, then the news it tells us is the most exciting, awe-inspiring, life-changing news that anyone could ever learn or hear. The Bible tells us that this short life on earth is intended to be only a taster, not the whole story. The whole story is available to anyone who will trust 100 per cent in Jesus Christ and his promises. For the special offer announced in the Bible is far more than the news that there is a God who loves you, who is willing to forgive your sins if you repent of them, and who wants to have a personal relationship with you now and forever. It is more than a promise to rescue you from everything that enslaves you, and to give you instead a new life filled with hope and joy and fulfilment. It is all that, it really is; yet it is far, far more than that.

The complete good news, beginning in the first chapter of the Bible and ending in the last one, is that the God who created this present world supernaturally some six thousand years ago is going to make another one. He is going to create a new earth, and this time it will be a world that is free from decay, disease, death and everything else that has been the result of sin. He will live in this renewed earth himself, in the person of his son Jesus Christ. Jesus will be king, and everyone who is willing to live under his kingship is invited to join him in that perfect kingdom to come. Here is how the Bible expresses this marvellous news:

> *...what we suffer now is nothing compared to the glory he will give us later. For all creation is waiting patiently and hopefully for that future day when God will resurrect his children. ... We, too, wait anxiously for that day when God will give us our full rights as his children, including the new bodies he has promised us—bodies that will never be sick again and will never die.*
>
> Romans 8.18,19,23 TLB

> *Then I saw a new heaven and a new earth; for the first heaven and the first earth had passed away, and the sea was no more... Death shall be*

Epilogue

> *no more, neither shall there be mourning nor crying nor pain any more, for the former things have passed away.*
>
> Revelation 21.1,4

And here's how Jesus's favourite disciple, John, expressed the heart of that promise in the same Bible:

> *...God loved the world so much that he gave his only Son so that anyone who believes in him shall not perish but have eternal life.*
>
> John 3.16 TLB

Your choice, your decision

That verse in John's Gospel offers you and me a simple choice. When we die, we can either perish or we can live forever. By believing in Jesus you can come back to life in a new body, just as Jesus did when he rose from the dead. You can live with Jesus forever in God's new creation and enjoy life in all its fullness, life as it was to begin with in the Garden of Eden, life as it was always intended to be.

Anyone who believes in him... The big question is, what does it mean to believe in Jesus?

When I was about seventeen years old I spent the first week of January with some other Scouts, climbing mountains in Snowdonia. A man named Len was assigned to be our guide. Towards the end of the week he made an unexpected announcement. He wanted to take us up Snowdon, the highest mountain in Wales, not by one of the easier routes but over the dreaded Crib Goch ridge. The ridge is a knife-edge of rock a mile long with a steep drop of 1000 feet (300 metres) on each side of it. Even experienced climbers have fallen to their deaths from Crib Goch, for the ridge is only a few feet wide along the top and there is little to hold on to. Worse than that, we were going to cross it in the depths of winter, when it was covered in deep snow!

We didn't have to go with Len. We had a choice. We could go with him, or spend the day back in the safety and warmth of the hostel in Llanberis. We knew that if we decided to trust Len to lead us safely over Crib Goch we'd have to follow his instructions to the letter! But of course we all went with him.

It was definitely frightening. When we reached the ridge some of the Scouts even chose to crawl much of the way through the snow on their hands and knees rather than risk standing upright! But somehow we all managed to follow Len safely to the summit. Standing on top of the pile of boulders that then crowned the highest peak in Wales we could see as far as Anglesey across the Menai Straits in the west, and to the north-east the Wirral and Liverpool on the far side of the River Dee. And what made us just as happy was that there was an easier way down and a hot meal awaiting us when we got there! Such an expedition would never be allowed in these days of enforced health and safety. It would have taken only one slip for someone to fall to his death that January.

Near the beginning of time it took Adam only one rebellious slip into sin to forfeit eternal life, both for himself and for the rest of the human race. (Romans 5.12) That's how serious sin is. All the troubles in this world are caused directly or indirectly by sin. And that is something which causes God pain too, intense pain, for he loves his creation, and people most of all. He must absolutely hate it when people kill each other in wars, or murder or steal or lie or rape, etc. So when he starts again with a new earth, this time he won't allow it to be spoilt by sin of any kind. And all that has one inevitable implication: there can be no sinners in it. (Revelation 21.27)

None of us is perfect, therefore if you and I are going to live in the kingdom to come we must be changed. Only one person has ever lived without sin, and he is the only one who can enable us to do the same. Only one person has ever defeated death, and he is the only one who can enable us to defeat it too. Only one person has always lived and will always live, and he is the only one who can truly offer us everlasting life in all its fullness. The name of that one person is Jesus Christ. *"...there is salvation in no one else, for there is no other name under heaven given among men by which we must be saved."* (Acts 4.12)

"I died, and behold I am alive for evermore." (Revelation 1.18) Jesus is alive now. His resurrection proved it, and his promises affirmed it. He is close to each one of us by his Spirit. He is close to you as you read this. To believe in him means to put your trust in him, just as we all put our trust in Len, our mountain guide. It means to put your trust in Jesus to save you from sin, to set you free from everything that would keep you out of the kingdom of God, and to give you eternal life. You don't have to earn this; you don't have to deserve it;

Epilogue

you don't have to be good enough—no one is. Instead you have to hand your life over to Jesus to be your Saviour and Lord, to follow his instructions implicitly, and to accept his help so that you can begin living with him now as your king, just as you will live when you come into his everlasting kingdom. He once died for you. Will you live for him?

It's your decision. You can make it right now.

Begin a new life here and now

Find somewhere quiet where you can talk aloud to Jesus. He has been longing for this moment since before you were born. Use your own words, or say the following prayer if it expresses what's in your heart.

> *Dear Lord Jesus,*
>   *I believe you are the Son of God. You know who I am. I realize that because of my sin I am under a death sentence. I am truly sorry for all the wrong things I have done and said and thought.* (If there's anything in particular on your conscience mention it.)
>   *Please forgive me. With your help I now want to live the way you want me to and to fulfil the purpose you made me for.*
> *Lord Jesus,*
>   *I thank you very much that you died on the cross so that I can be forgiven and set free from sin to live forever in your kingdom.*
>   *I now open the door of my life to you. Please come in as my saviour and Lord, and help me to live for you from this moment onwards.*
>   *Thank you, Lord Jesus.*

Jesus said, *"All that the Father gives me will come to me; and him who comes to me I will not cast out."* (John 6.37) If you prayed like that and meant it you can be confident that Jesus has accepted you and restored you to a right relationship with the Father; that all your sins have been forgiven and that you have the promise of everlasting life.

If we confess our sins, he is faithful and just, and will forgive our sins and cleanse us from all unrighteousness.

1 John 1.9

God, Science and the Bible

> *"...this is the will of my Father, that every one who sees the Son and believes in him should have eternal life; and I will raise him up at the last day."*
>
> John 6.40

What a great promise!

The Bible says that when we believe in Jesus to save us and receive him as lord of our life, we become a child of God. (John 1.12) Here are some suggestions for your first steps as God's new son or daughter.

<u>Make a permanent note of the date.</u>

It's your new birthday! You'll want to remember this day in the future.

> *When someone becomes a Christian, he becomes a brand new person inside. He is not the same any more. A new life has begun!*
>
> 2 Corinthians 5.17 TLB

Making a note of the date is like inscribing the date a building is started on the foundation stone. God is going to build something amazing out of you!

<u>Tell someone what you have done.</u>

> *For if you tell others with your own mouth that Jesus Christ is your Lord and believe in your own heart that God has raised him from the dead, you will be saved.*
>
> Romans 10.9 TLB

Telling someone is like cementing the foundation stone in place.

<u>Be baptized.</u>

> *Those who believe and are baptized will be saved.*
>
> Mark 16.16 TLB

In the Bible baptism means being immersed in water by the leaders of a church. It is a way of making public your decision to belong to Jesus, just as a wedding is a way of making public a decision to share one's life with someone else permanently. Baptism

Epilogue

doesn't 'save' you, but it's how you show Jesus that you are willing to obey him, and how he assures you that your sins have been washed away and your new life with him has truly begun. It is God's appointed way for making your union with his Son final, public and permanent.

To be baptized you will have to find a church if you don't already belong to one. Churches can be big or small, formal or informal, dead or alive. A good local church will welcome you into God's family and help you to grow as a child of God. Do an Internet search for 'Lively church in Marshmere-under-Water / Little Grumbling / Dancing-by-the-Sea' or wherever you live, to find what's available. If several churches are listed, ask God to guide you and try visiting two or three of them on Sundays until you feel that you have found one that could become your spiritual home. Make sure they do proper baptisms!

Receive the Holy Spirit.

Ask God to fill you with his Holy Spirit, or ask the church leaders at your baptism to pray that he will.

> *"…if even sinful persons like yourselves give children what they need, don't you realize that your heavenly Father will do at least as much, and give the Holy Spirit to those who ask for him?"*
>
> Luke 11.13 TLB

You have to ask!
The Holy Spirit gives us the power to live as God wants us to.

> *…those who follow after the Holy Spirit find themselves doing those things that please God.*
>
> Romans 8.5 TLB

Find a mentor.

If you already have a Christian friend, ask if he or she would be willing to meet you on a regular basis for a while, to help you to learn how to follow Jesus. If you don't have such a friend, ask if there is someone in the church who would like to help you in this way.

Talk to your heavenly Father each day.

Find a quiet place to pray and follow the TSP 'teaspoon rule':

1. Thank God for anything that comes to your mind.
2. Tell him you are *sorry* for any way you've failed him and ask him to forgive you.
3. Ask him please to help you and anyone else you know who is in need.

<u>Read the Bible.</u>

The Bible is like food for your spirit. It will enable you to grow into a strong Christian. If you don't have a Bible of your own you can download one as an app, or else you can buy an electronic or physical copy. There are different kinds of English translation. Search for 'Bibles for new believers' for guidance on the translation that would best suit you.[131]

Annex 2 provides a useful list of Bible readings suitable for new Christians.

Ideally, set aside a time each day when you can read a passage of the Bible, think about it, and perhaps even make some notes on what you learn in a notebook or journal. My wife and I used to read it together each morning in bed before we got up, and then we prayed about what we had read, as well as anything else that was on our minds.

Enjoy your new life as a citizen of heaven. And do introduce yourself to me when we meet in the resurrection!

~~~~~~

Folk hesitate to buy a book that no one else has read,
But if it has a good review then they will go ahead!

If possible, write a few sentences of review on this book's page at Amazon or another online bookseller's website. Did you like the book, what was your favourite or most helpful part, and who would you recommend it to?

If God has spoken to you through *God, Science and the Bible*, please recommend it to your friends.

---

[131] At the time of writing, one website providing guidance on the best Bibles for different kinds of people was eden.co.uk's Eden's Top 5 Bibles for New Believers.

Epilogue

Visit my website www.booksforlife.today for a free book: *The Way, the Truth and the Life, 21 simple Bible studies for new Christians.*

My book *The Date of Christ's Return—Biblical prophecy in the final generation* explains fully what is going to happen before and after the promised return of Jesus Christ, and how we can be ready for this.

I am always willing to consider requests to speak on a subject covered by my books. Email brief details and a telephone number to: info@booksforlife.today.

Follow me at:
TikTok: @arnoldpageauthor
Facebook: @booksforlifetoday
Blog: www.booksforlife.today/blog.php

God, Science and the Bible

ANNEX 1

Seven Days of Expanding Time

In this annex I propose a theory which to some extent resolves the conflict between the Bible's statement that it took six literal days to create the universe and most scientists' insistence that it took 13.8 billion years. Personally I believe that the Bible's account of creation is literally true for the reasons I have explained, but if you still can't believe that God could make everything in six days of current time this might help you to believe the biblical account, provided that you have some knowledge of science and maths. I honestly don't know if my theory makes any sense to a physicist, but I feel it's worth a shot, and it does seem possible to verify it to some extent, as you will read.

According to the Big Bang theory as I understand it, space expanded to accommodate all the material exploding from a single point of origin. In other words, space was created at the same time as matter was released. Initially space expanded very fast, but the rate of expansion decreased as time passed. However time is meaningless unless time was also created along with space. So let's suppose that time was also very compressed to start with and that it expanded rapidly at first and then gradually slowed down. What would that mean?

It would mean that in the beginning, each second would take far less than a second now takes. So during one of our present seconds, an enormous number of original seconds would initially have passed, enabling an awful lot to happen in that time. To us it would seem as though everything happened much faster than it does now.

Imagine another planet just like ours, except that everything in it happened ten times as fast as it does on the earth. In a day of our time, the inhabitants could achieve ten times as much as we can. On another planet where everything happened a hundred times as fast, the inhabitants could achieve a hundred times as much as we can in a day of our time.

I propose that initially time, like space, was infinitely compressed. Initially it expanded infinitely 'fast' but its rate of expansion decreased exponentially, until by the end of seven days of our current time it was more or less the same as time is now. This would mean that a great deal could have happened in the first day, and less and less as each day passed.

Crucially, it would mean that in the time it takes for seven of our current 24-hour days to pass, many, many more real days would have passed while the universe was being formed. In fact it could have taken 13.8 billion years of current time for the work to be completed in six days. Hence creation could have taken place in six genuine days of current time, yet be 13.8 billion years old. Let's examine this idea more closely.

In Genesis we have the following sequence of creation:

Day 1—light
Day 2—the earth's atmosphere
Day 3—separation of land and sea, and the creation of vegetation and trees
Day 4—sun, moon and stars
Day 5—fish and birds
Day 6—animals, reptiles, etc., and people

This doesn't conform to any natural sequence—light before sun, and trees before stars!—so even with a theory of expanding time one cannot reconcile the Genesis account with any natural account of the creation of the world.

However, the order of events would appear more natural if the creation of the sun, moon and stars took place on Day 2 rather than on Day 4, and the subsequent events took place a day later. If this was the order in which God originally told Moses he had made things, the current order in Genesis might have been changed on purpose by a scribe who believed that the earth was the centre of the universe and that it must therefore have been created before the sun, moon and stars were. If we make this single amendment to the

Annex 1

current order of events in Genesis it appears to be much more natural.

Assuming a decreasing exponential rate of time expansion, the following formula will produce a decrease from 13.8 billion years for the generally accepted age of the universe to 6000 years over a period of seven days.

$$[6000 \times (8-n)]^{7.53} \text{ where } n \text{ is the day number}$$

Hence, entering into the formula values of n from 1 to 7 for each day of creation we obtain the following apparent ages for each stage of creation:

n	Calculated age	Event in Genesis chapter 1
1	13.8 billion	Light, energy, space and time began 13.8 billion years ago.
2	4.32 billion	Sun, moon and stars were created 4.32 billion years ago.
3	1.09 billion	Earth's atmosphere was created 1.09 billion years ago.
4	204 million	Separation of land and sea, creation of vegetation and trees.
5	23.4 million	Fish and birds created.
6	1.11 million	Animals, reptiles etc., and humans created.
7	6.0 thousand	God rested from his work of creation 6000 years ago.

With these calculated ages for each stage of creation, the theory can be tested against the estimated ages of the listed events as commonly accepted. For instance the age assigned to the formation of the solar system is generally 4.53 billion years. That is very close to the 4.32 billion years predicted by the formula.

Other ages listed in Wikipedia's 'Timeline of evolutionary history of life' are as follows:

- fish   450 to 400 million years ago
- land plants   360 to 220 million
- reptiles   225 to 100 million

- animals   170 to 4 million
- birds   110 to 25 million
- humans   2 to 0.25 million.

Table A.1 compares the age of each stage of creation as calculated by my formula with its generally accepted age as listed above. With the exception of fish the two sets of data match remarkably closely.

Table A.1: Comparison of calculated and accepted dates for the formation of the world

Stage		Years ago		Original day number in Genesis
n	Description	Wikipedia article on the evolutionary history of life	Predicted by formula $6000 \times (8-n)^{7.527}$	
1	'Big bang'	13.8 billion	13.8 billions	1[b]
2	Solar system	4.530 billion	4.320 billion	4[c]
3	Earth's atmosphere	4.500 to 1.000 billions	1.090 billion	2
4	Vegetation and trees	360 to 35 million	204 million	3
5	Birds	110 to 25 million	23.4 million	5
6	Reptiles, animals and man	225 to 0.25 million	1.11 million	6
7	God rested	n/a	6000	7
3.5[e]	Fish	450 to 400 million	495 million	5

[a] Matched to scientific estimate, so not predicted.
[b] Equating "Let there be light!" with the Big Bang.
[c] The formula would match the account in Genesis only if Genesis had the sun, moon and stars created on Day 2 and the things created on Day 2 and 3 moved to Day 3 and 4. See the explanation in the main text.
[d] 4.500 billion first atmosphere, 1.000 billion formation of oxygen.
[e] In order to match the evolutionary date given to fish, we have to assume that fish were created midway between Days 3 and 4, instead of on Day 5 as the Bible says.

Annex 1

Apart from the fish date, my predicted dates based on a revised order of events in Genesis match the generally *accepted* scientific dates pretty well. They match very well indeed the scientific dates for the cosmological events that preceded the supposed emergence of life. And as I explained in Chapter 7, the dates commonly assigned by scientists to the emergence of various life forms are based on very dubious evidence. If palaeontologists were to announce in the future that the first fish appeared much later than they originally thought, in fact at much the same time as birds, it would add immense credence to my little theory and perhaps even make me famous!

Personally I take the Bible's account of creation at its face value, so I'm not at all convinced that my theory is true. The universe could only have been created supernaturally, as I explained in Chapter 2, and if God created it supernaturally then he could have done it in any period of time he chose, even instantaneously.

Nevertheless, it would be very nice if my little theory were true. It would explain why I never seem to achieve so much in a day as I used to. It's not because I am growing old: it's because time is still expanding!

God, Science and the Bible

ANNEX 2

Fifty-day Bible-reading Plan

Reproduced by permission of Shoreline Community Church, Monterey, California.

Every Bible has an index to its various books at the front. A reference like 'John 1.1-18' means the book of John, chapter 1, verses 1 to 18. Don't confuse 'John', the book of John, with '1 John', the first letter of John.

The Story of the Christian Faith (New Testament)

Day 1. Luke chapters 1 & 2: The birth of Jesus
Day 2. John 1:1–18: The identity of Jesus
Day 3. Luke 4:14–44: Jesus begins his ministry
Day 4. Matthew 5 & 6: The core of Jesus's teachings
Day 5. John 3: God's love for the world
Day 6. John 5: Jesus's miracles and authority
Day 7. John 11: Jesus's power over death
Day 8. John 15: The Christian life defined
Day 9. Matthew 26 & 27: The arrest and crucifixion of Jesus
Day 10. John 20 & Luke 24: The resurrection of Jesus and his ascension
Day 11. Acts 2: The coming of the Holy Spirit
Day 12. Acts 9:1–19: The conversion of Saul and his ministry
Day 13. Acts 26: Paul's defence of the Christian faith
Day 14. Romans 3: Justification by faith alone
Day 15. Romans 7 & 8: The battle with sin, and life in the Spirit
Day 16. 1 Corinthians 13, Ephesians 5: The way of love
Day 17. 1 Corinthians 15: The power of the resurrection

Day 18. Galatians 5, Ephesians 4: Freedom and unity in Christ
Day 19. Ephesians 6: The whole armour of God
Day 20. Philippians 1:18 to 2:18: Christ's example
Day 21. Colossians 3:1–17: Putting on the new self
Day 22. Hebrews 4:14 to 5:10: Jesus the great high priest
Day 23. James 1 & 1 Peter 1: Pure religion
Day 24. 1 John 4:7–21: God is love
Day 25. Revelation 21 & 22: The new heaven and earth

Old Testament survey

Day 26. Genesis 1:1 to 3:19: The creation and fall of humanity
Day 27. Genesis 12; 28:10–15; 32:22–28: God calls a people his
Day 28. Genesis 37; 39 to 46: The story of Joseph
Day 29. Exodus 1 to 6: The call of Moses
Day 30. Exodus 7 to 14: Moses and Pharaoh
Day 31. Exodus 19:1 to 20:20: The Ten Commandments
Day 32. Deuteronomy 6:1 to 7:26; 11:13–21: Obedience flows
Day 33. Judges 1:1 to 2:19: Cycles of disobedience in God's people
Day 34. 1 Samuel 7 to 9; 15 to 17: The fall of Saul and rise of David
Day 35. 2 Samuel 5; 7 to 9; 11 & 12: Tales of David's life
Day 36. 1 Kings 2 & 3; 6; 11: Solomon's reign
Day 37. 1 Kings 11:9 to 14:31: The dividing of the kingdom
Day 38. 1 Kings 17 to 19; 2 Kings 2 & 4: The prophets Elijah and Elisha
Day 39. Job 1 & 2; 38 to 42: How the righteous respond to hard times
Day 40. Psalms 1; 23; 139: Psalms that enrich your soul
Day 41. Psalms 6; 22; 38; 51: Psalms for the suffering and sinful
Day 42. Proverbs 3; 5; 7; 16; 31: Wisdom for everyday life
Day 43. Jeremiah 11 &12; 31:31–40: The covenant broken and
Day 44. Jeremiah 23:1–6; Isaiah 9:6,7; 53:1–12: Jesus the promised king
Day 45. Jonah 1 to 4: The story of Jonah
Day 46. Daniel 1 to 3: Exile in Babylon
Day 47. Daniel 4 to 6: The life of Daniel

Annex 2

Day 48. Nehemiah 1 & 2; 4 & 5; 8 & 9: The rebuilding of Jerusalem
Day 49. Esther 1 to 8: The story of Esther
Day 50. Malachi 1 to 4: Final words of the Old Testament

Further help can be found in *Every Day with Jesus for New Christians*, published by the Crusade for World Revival as a small paperback and as an e-book.

God, Science and the Bible

Other books by Arnold V Page

Twenty-first Century Nutrition and Family Health

This important book explains what is wrong with current recommendations for healthy eating and provides clear guidance on a truly healthy diet and lifestyle. It is supported by references to over 500 peer-reviewed scientific papers and similar publications. The author's wife was taken off thirteen years of medication for Type 2 diabetes when the recommended diet corrected her blood sugar level. The author at the age of 70 climbed all sixteen peaks in Snowdonia over 3000 feet high in 24 hours.

Available from www.booksforlife.today.

I'm very impressed. Brilliant!   Dr David Walton, MBBS

The following books are available from all major booksellers.

The Date of Christ's Return—Biblical Prophecy in the Final Generation

What does the future hold for Generation Z, the current crop of children and young people? Nothing less than the most exciting event in history! In this controversial and powerfully argued book, science researcher and Bible teacher Arnold V Page contends that Z, the final letter of the alphabet, will also be the final generation that grows to adulthood before Jesus Christ returns to establish justice, peace and righteousness throughout the earth.

It provides a full explanation of Biblical prophecy on the subject.

(Also available in Spanish.)

A fascinating and remarkable portrayal of the world's entire timeline in one cohesive, panoramic form, from a Biblical perspective. Regardless of your religion/value system, I would urge you to read this book.

From a review by Raju Chacko for Reedsy.com

Tell me about the Holy Spirit

God, Science and the Bible

If the fruit of the Spirit is love, joy, peace, patience, kindness, goodness, faithfulness, gentleness and self-control, where is it? What does it mean to be filled with the Spirit, and how does it happen? Can we demonstrate more effectively the reality, power and love of God to people we meet by living more supernaturally? *Tell me about the Holy Spirit* provides the Bible's answers to such questions. It will show you how to fly!

So many claim to have received the Holy Spirit, yet lack any real evidence. This book will help them to find what they are searching for.

Rev. D Hathaway. President Eurovision Mission to Europe

The Destiny of the Damned

"How can a God of love deliberately torment unbelievers forever in hell, especially if they have never heard of Jesus?" That is a question many Christian writers fail to address. In this book, Arnold V Page faces it head on by showing from the pages of Scripture that God will do no such a thing, and that while severe punishment does await deliberate unbelievers in God on the Day of Judgement, everlasting torment will not be their fate. Indeed, some who have never had the opportunity to believe in Jesus Christ will have their names written in the Book of Life.

The question of judgement of those that don't ever hear the Gospel message is clearly covered. I'm so pleased to have this pamphlet to share with Christians and non Christians.

David Lloyd, Amazon reviewer

Unearthly Passion (A novel for GenZ by Vincy Page)

Unwanted and unloved as a child, Natalie Parsons longs to escape from the moral restraints of her foster family and embark on a life of boozing and floozing at Edinburgh University. Her first-year geophysics course finds her rebelling against the idea that the universe, like herself, originated as a meaningless accident. Jettisoning her moral compass, she sinks ever deeper into drink, debt and sexual depravity, until the break-up of a relationship with a lecturer lands her in a life-threatening depression. Rescue comes through a friend who claims to know God, producing a dilemma that only a miracle

Other Books by Arnold V Page

can solve. Will Natalie ever find the one thing that can make sense of her life—true love?

Brazen T-shirts and outrageous tattoos enliven a humorous and emotional roller coaster of a story that explores the origin of the universe, the truth about God and a reason for living.

"Uplifting through its powerful lessons."
Edith Wairimu, ReadersFavorite.com.

"I only wish that every pastor, parent, teacher, social worker and indeed anyone interested in truth and morality, as I am, would read this excellent book."
Rev G R Hargrove, JP

Tell Them I'm Real—Real life miracles of God's love from England to Chile and back

What happens when you say yes to God—even when you don't know where it will lead? When a series of divine visions called Arnold and his wife Ann to uproot their lives and take their young children to South America, their faith would be tested in ways they never imagined.

Follow their journey through doubt and deliverance, through prayers whispered into silence and others answered in breathtaking, miraculous ways. As Arnold wrestles to obey God's will—the delays, the detours, the heartbreak—he discovers a deep truth: that God knows what he is doing, even when nothing seems to make sense.

Whether you're searching for evidence of God's reality or simply longing to feel his closeness again, this honest, hope-filled account will both challenge and encourage you.

"It took me from laugh-out-loud episodes to shedding heart-breaking tears of sorrow, and moments of total wonder along the way. This is one of my favourite books from this year."
Rachel Yarworth, Author and Blogger

~~~~~~

Register at booksforlife.today for news of release dates, pre-release review copies and a free copy of *The Way, the Truth and the Life*.

www.ingramcontent.com/pod-product-compliance
Lightning Source LLC
Chambersburg PA
CBHW050247120526
44590CB00016B/2249